Joris-Karl Huysmans (1848-1907) published two overlapping collections of prose poems, *Le drageoir aux épices* (1874) and *Croquis Parisiens*, producing two Naturalist novels, *Marthe* (1876) and *Les Soeurs Vatard* (1879) in between. *À rebours* (1884) represented a dramatic change of direction, and became the handbook of Decadent lifestyle fantasy. *Là-Bas* (1891), based on the author's flirtation with the Parisian Occult Revival, became equally archetypal in its fascinated but horrified account of contemporary Satanism.

SNUGGLY BOOKS

J.-K. HUYSMANS

THE CROWDS
OF LOURDES

TRANSLATED BY W. H. MITCHELL

THE CROWDS
OF LOURDES

INTRODUCTION

I HAVE no intention of telling in detail the story of Bernadette and of Lourdes. Hundreds of books have done that. Over and over again what might be called the rigmarole has been recapitulated by pens belonging to all parties; it has been worn threadbare by repetition. I merely propose, for the better understanding of the sketches and notes which compose this book, briefly to recall the apparitions of the Virgin in the grotto of Massabielle, on the borders of the Gave, to the west of Lourdes.

In 1858 the Virgin appeared eighteen times—from Thursday, February 11, till Friday, July 16—to a little girl of fourteen—the eldest of the six children of the miller François Soubirous—to Bernadette.

Bernadette saw her in a sort of luminous mist, standing in a lancet-pointed cleft riven high up in the rock. She looked like a maiden of sixteen or seventeen, of medium height, or rather under it, very pretty, with a sweet voice and blue eyes. She was clad in a white robe, caught in at the waist with a sky-blue sash falling in two bands down to her bare feet, hidden by the bottom of her garment except at the toes; and on these flowered a yellow rose, all aflame. Her head was covered with a veil, and in her hands was a rosary of white beads threaded on a golden chain.

In her various apparitions She spoke in the Lourdes dialect, and said to the child:

"Will you kindly come here for a fortnight? . . . I do not promise to make you happy in this world, but in the world to come. . . . Pray to God for sinners. . . . Penance, penance, penance. . . . Go and tell the priests to build a chapel here. . . . I want people to come here in procession. . . . Go and drink of the spring and wash in it: go and eat of the grass you find there. . . . I am the Immaculate Conception; I desire a chapel here."

Besides this, she revealed to Bernadette a special form of prayer and three personal secrets which were never divulged.

Let us add that the Virgin, at the moment of speaking, did not create the spring which melts away as it spreads from the grotto: it had long been there, but it was invisible and was flowing, unknown to all, beneath the sand before proceeding doubtless to disappear in the course of the Gave. Hence the Virgin confined herself to pointing its place out to the little maid, and this led her to scrape the earth away and make it gush forth.

This spring, when it first broke from the ground, was a mere thread no thicker than a finger, but it now yields over forty thousand gallons a day and never runs dry.

It has become famous for the cures of which it has been a vehicle.

As for Bernadette, after suffering all kinds of trials inflicted on her by authorities ecclesiastical and civil, when her mission was over at the age of twenty-two she entered the Convent of St Gildard of the Sisters of Charity at Nevers. There she took the veil as Sister Marie Bernard and died a very holy death on April 16, 1879, aged thirty-five years, three months and nine days.

I

THE apparitions of the Blessed Virgin in our own times have nothing about them to fill us with surprise. In the history of France Lourdes is neither an exception nor a novelty: the Mother of Christ has always regarded France as her fief. Never, except in the eighteenth century, has She deprived it of the continual boon of her presence; but if we bear in mind the astounding baseness of the Bourbons and the inexorable infamy of the Jacobins, that exception is easily explained.

We had to wait even to the end of the first half of the nineteenth century to see her reappearing to some privileged souls in certain specially reserved corners of her domains.

The last of her indubitable apparitions, that of Lourdes, is then only in line with her earlier manifestations; hence I think it is peculiarly interesting to give a plain summary of those that went before it.

They spring from two sources: the one purely regional; the other Parisian.

The precedents of Lourdes in the region of the Pyrenees are numerous. If you take a map of the dioceses of Bayonne and Tarbes, you can draw a circle round Lourdes with the hamlets and chapels which were formerly centres for pilgrimages of our Lady; and then Lourdes will appear in the middle of the ring as a living planet surrounded with nine satellites well-nigh dead.

These satellites are:

Notre-Dame de Héas;
Notre-Dame de Piétat, at Barbazan;
Notre-Dame de Piétat, at Saint-Savin;
Notre-Dame de Poueylahün;
Notre-Dame de Bourisp;
Notre-Dame de Nestès;
Notre-Dame de Médoux;
Notre-Dame de Bétharram;
Notre-Dame de Garaison.

All these sanctuaries, except the last but one, which belongs to the bishopric of Bayonne, depend upon the diocese of Tarbes.

Here I give the story of each one, sketched in a few lines:

Notre-Dame de Héas, high up in a village between Baréges and Saint-Sauveur, was in existence before the sixteenth century, for it is mentioned in a deed of 1415. The chapel is said to have been founded by the family of Estrade d'Esquièze to enable shepherds lost in the pasture-lands to hear Mass on Sundays. Today it is sometimes visited by tourists who have been lured on to climb the mountains on the crest of which it is perched.

Notre-Dame de Piétat. The origin of this chapel, situate at Barbazan, is lost in the dim distance of past ages, and records of its life, now finished, are wanting. The other Notre-Dame de Piétat at Saint-Savin, rose above the Benedictine Abbey of that name, and was built by a hermit of Poitou who still has an altar in the abbey church of Ligugé.

His relics, contained in an ancient reliquary which dealers in antiques hanker after, rest in the village church of Saint-Savin, where, by the way is an old broken down and highly curious medieval organ. When the pedals are depressed they set in motion the jaws of fantastic heads which thrust out their tongues at the flock. These grotesques, whose grimaces in a church are so astonishing, are gaily carved and their colouring is violent.

Notre-Dame de Poueylahün, at Arrens, is dominated on all sides by high mountains; her chapel is built in Renaissance style; formerly the Virgin was widely venerated there, but now she is honoured only by the good women of the neighbourhood; as for her records, they are nil.

Notre-Dame de Bourisp, at Vieille-Aure, arose from the legends so often told by medieval historians of an ox discovering and worshipping a statue of the Madonna, who is borne about to various places and always returns miraculously to the spot where she was dug out, and thus compels the people to build her a church just where she wants to have it. This statue is said to date from the twelfth century. In France it is now venerated only by the faithful of Vieille-Aure.

Notre Dame de Nestès, at Montoussé. The Site of this church, like that of St Mary Major in Rome, was designated by a sheet of snow falling from the sky at midsummer. It was in a state of ruin, and had long been abandoned until, in June, 1848, amidst a thorn bush growing out of a heap of stones, three little girls saw a luminous statue of the Virgin. Then it was decided to rebuild the chapel and therein to replace the old statue which had been taken over in 1793 by the parish church of the town. Except the neighbouring country folk, none of the faithful now resort thither, and it is unknown to pilgrims.

Notre-Dame de Médoux, about a mile and a half to the South of Bagnères-de-Bigorre, opposite the hamlet of Asté, owed its vogue, now over and done with, to two legends.

The first partly recalls the legend of Notre-Dame de Bourisp. It has no ox, but once more we get the statue returning of its own accord to the sanctuary from which it had been taken. In fact, the inhabitants of Bagnères-de-Bigorre took possession of it in 1562, and put it on a cart to be carried away to their town, but, on reaching the little bridge over the Martinet, it broke its bonds and clove the air to get back to its own church.

The second is more interesting and more recent. In 1648 the Virgin appeared to a poor shepherdess named Liloye, who was praying before her image, and bade her warn the clergy and the people of Bagneres to do penance for their sins. Liloye delivered this message in vain and returned, flouted, to the Virgin, who renewed her orders and declared that, if they were not attended to, she would decimate the town with a dreadful plague.

Liloye obeyed once more, but her warnings went for nothing; then the plague raged and slew all those who were unable to escape. Bagneres was deserted for a year; and then the guilty, who had avoided the scourge by withdrawing from the infected town, gradually returned. One of the women who had left the place, a certain Simone de Souville, met Liloye in the street and said to her jeeringly: "The providential epidemic you predicted for us could only catch those who were so unfortunate as to have no means of slipping away; but the rest of us have been able to escape it quite easily. So your lesson is not as perfect as it might be, and we shall expect less maladroit warnings before we are converted."

"Go," thereupon said the Virgin to Liloye, "go and warn the black sheep that the scourge shall next smite the rich, and that she will be the first victim."

And the prediction was fulfilled to the letter, and Simone died.

The people were terrified and repented, and numerous processions filed year after year past the altar dedicated to our Lady. As for Liloye, she became a nun in the Convent of Balbonne, near Mont-serrat in Spain, for all the religious houses of her own country had been burnt by the Huguenots.

This sanctuary at Médoux served by the Capuchins, amongst whom was Fr. Anthony de Lombez who died in the odour of sanctity in 1778, became famous for its Pyrenean pilgrimages. Cures and all sorts of other miracles drew crowds of pilgrims; and then came the Revolution and drove them away, so the chapel was closed and the statue transferred to the parish church.

Notre-Dame de Bétharram is situated in the village of that name which is linked up by the railway with Lourdes. This now makes one of the best-known excursions for pilgrims who go there to spend a few hours and to give their piety a change of air. Built no one knows when in consequence of a miracle which, except that they were shepherds instead of little shepherdesses who discovered a luminous statue of the Virgin in a bush, recalls almost word for word the legend of Notre-Dame de Nèstes, the church was burnt down by the Protestants in 1569, but the statue was recovered from the fire unharmed, and saved by a priest who carried it off to Tauste, near Saragossa in Spain, where it should still be found.

The church remained nothing but a heap of ruins, and nevertheless cures of the incurable were still wrought there, and crowds thronged thither to invoke the Virgin.

Louis XIII restored the sanctuary and Leonard de Trappes, Archbishop of Auch, put up a new statue in it on July 14, 1616, to replace the one which the people of Tauste refused to restore; and, on the eve of the Assumption in 1622, a fountain which had run dry years ago began to flow in abundance in a little grotto near the church, and many miracles were worked by means of the water, as if the Madonna wanted to give an anticipation of the cures she was to work by the same means two centuries later on at Lourdes.

The church to be seen there today recalls both the Renaissance style and that of the Jesuits as it appears at Antwerp; and it is worth visiting. The interior is fantastic with arches carried on very low pillars, about as tall as a man, great angels carved in wood and gilt, cut off at half-length, like the mythological busts of the Termini, and from the waist upwards garlanded with foliage of rose-trees and oaks. The altar is an enormous raised piece of work, gilded along all the seams, supported on twisted columns wreathed with vine-branches, and decorated with doves, angels and naked chubby Cupids in the style of Rubens, surrounding a placid and impassive effigy of the Virgin. The nave, surmounted by a vaulted ceiling of wood painted sky-blue, is decorated with naïve pictures telling of the miracles lately wrought, and, in a chapel on the right, a bas-relief recounts the episode of the apparition to the shepherds of Mary smiling in a burning bush.

Her Ladyship of the manor, who scattered the alms of her favours so freely of yore in her mansion at Bétharram, has moved house and fixed her abode farther away in the aforesaid spot of Massabielle.

These various pilgrimages may thus be considered as the antecedents of the hyperdulical triumphs of Lourdes, but their legends, lost in the night of the past, only resemble the history of the Grotto in certain points. At most we can but regard Liloye as a rough draft of Bernadette, for, after having acted as the Virgin's interpreter and undergone the contradictions of a whole town, she ended her life, as did the daughter of Soubirous, in a cloister; and, on the other hand, the spring and grotto of Bétharram are to some extent the forerunners of Lourdes

In the case of Notre-Dame de Garaison, the points of resemblance come out more clearly and are more definite; for here we find everything—the shepherd-ess, the grotto, the water, the countless crowds coming from all sorts of quarters, and the miracles and cures. It may indeed be said that in the sixteenth and seven-teenth centuries this pilgrimage was what the Lourdes pilgrimage is in our own days.

The story of Notre-Dame de Garaison can be told in a few lines.

About the year 1500, at Monléon in the vale of Garaison, in a place formerly called "Goat's Moor," be-cause it was the rendezvous of the sorcerers of Gascony, Anglèse of Sagazan, a little shepherdess, was looking after her father's flocks near a spring, when a Lady in white clothing appeared to her, and, after making her-self known as the Virgin Mary asked—just as she did at Lourdes—for a chapel to be built for her and for processions to be made there.

The little girl ran to tell her father the news. He believed at once in her story, but it was not so with the neighbours, who shrugged their shoulders and laughed outright. Next day the child returned to the spring, and the Virgin again appeared to her and repeated her request, but the rectors and consuls of Monléon were convinced that both father and daughter must be mad to spin such yarns, and sent them off, bidding them to put themselves under care.

A third time Anglèse went to the spring, but she took her family and a few neighbours along with her. These people, however, did not see the Virgin when she did, but they all heard our Lady say that, to convince them, she was going to change the piece of black bread in the little girl's bag, as well as what was stored in the bread-pan at home, into very white loaves of bread. And both miracles took place, and the little town, despite its former unbelief, turned fervent: immediately processions were arranged; a chapel was built, but soon proved too small to hold the crowds which flocked in from all parts; it was pulled down in 1536, and a vast Gothic church was built in its place.

A wooden statue of Our Lady of Sorrows was placed on the high altar; and whence comes this statue, today worm-eaten and maggot-riddled, and presenting us with the likeness of a Virgin both dolorous and pensive, holding on her knees the lifeless body of her Son? No one knows. According to one legend, this Pietà was discovered, after hints from the Virgin, by Anglèse; according to another, it was dug out from under a thorn bush. Be its origin what it may, it was before it that conversions and cures of incurable diseases followed one upon another. The sick were brought from afar, and the blind saw and the lame walked after drinking of the water drawn from the spring. There came a check during the days of the League: the heretics plundered the church and threw the statue of our Lady into the fire, but, like the one thrown into the flames at Bétharram, it was not burnt. When the terror was over the crowds once more wended their way to Monléon, and they brought such prosperity to the town that the inhabitants were undone—just as those of Lourdes will be. Money gave rise to avarice and stirred up licentiousness, and the Virgin withdrew.

Garaison was just like any other place when the Revolution transformed the church into a powder factory; the Virgin's statue which had escaped the fury of the Jacobins was transferred to the parish church, and in 1834 the Bishop of Tarbes restored the sanctuary, and, in order to serve it, founded an association of missionaries from which came the Fathers of Lourdes.

The church is still frequented by the inhabitants of the district and by a few tourists.

As for Anglèse, in 1536 she went into the Cistercian monastery of Fabas, in the diocese of Comminges, about eighteen miles from Garaison. Tradition says that she presented herself three times, just as she had done to the Virgin, at the gate of the Abbey, the nuns of which belonged to the nobility of the neighbourhood. On the first two occasions she was shown out owing to her roughness, but the third time the gates opened of their own accord, and the bells spontaneously rang out a full peal. She was then admitted at once, and there she died over a hundred years old in the odour of sanctity—a simple nun, unable to read or write according to some; prioress according to others—on the eve of the Nativity of the Blessed Virgin Mary, in the year of our Lord 1589.

Lourdes, then, as we see, is not an isolated instance in the annals of the Pyrenees. It is but the revival of old popular devotions which have been rejuvenated by the Madonna: without any change of district She has restricted herself to transferring her abode to a site within easier reach of the devotion of crowds.

Such are the regional antecedents. The Parisian connection is less straightforward but it can be traced indirectly.

It is derived from Notre-Dame des Victoires which is linked with the chapel of the Sisters of St Vincent de Paul which again is connected across the ages with Saint-Séverin.

It must not be forgotten, indeed, that if Mary came to Lourdes to call sinners to do penance and by her cures to confirm the mediatory power of her grace, She Came also and above all to bear witness that she was that "Immaculate Conception" which had been defined as a dogma four years previously by Pope Pius IX, in Rome.

Now, in her previous apparitions in the Pyrenees, there had never been any question of this prerogative, of which She had never herself spoken before 1830, when She recalled it to one of the forerunners of Bernadette, to Catherine Labouré in Paris.

Thus, it was in this city that She first spoke to a human being of the inviolability of her birth.

Truth to tell, even in the time of Charlemagne, in various provinces of France Christians honoured the spotless Conception of the Virgin, and the University of Paris in the thirteenth century followed in this matter the teaching of St Anselm; but we had to wait until the fourteenth century to find a church in Paris erecting an altar and inaugurating a confraternity under the very name of the Immaculate Conception, and it was the church of Saint-Séverin which was the first in that city to recognise and celebrate, by those very acts, Mary's privilege.

This devotion was rewarded by the Virgin. She healed multitudes of the sick who often travelled from afar to drink the water of the well sunk at the foot of her statue.

But, as years passed by, the devotion fell off; Saint-Séverin ended by becoming once more a parish church rather than a shrine for pilgrims. In the seventeenth and eighteenth centuries it became a rendezvous for the Jansenists, and many years and many efforts were needed to uproot the sect from that quarter. Today the Virgin so despised by "Appellants"[1] has reinstated her dwelling-place, but if she still dispenses spiritual favours in it, she has apparently shut her dispensary, so far as bodily healing is concerned, along with the disuse of the well which her priests have closed.

---

1 The Appellants were a party of ecclesiastics in the beginning of the eighteenth century who *appealed* against the bull *Unigenitus* to the next Council.

In a word, during the fourteenth century devotion to the Immaculate Conception was very much alive in Paris; it lessened or rather got frittered away day by day during the Middle Ages; in later times it had no special abode, but lived from hand to mouth everywhere and nowhere, when, in November, 1830, the Virgin suddenly decided to give it a new impulse and to spread it not only in Paris but throughout the world.

It was then that she appeared to Catherine Labouré in the chapel of the Sisters of Charity, called the Grey Sisters of the Rue du Bac, and bade her have a medal struck for the purpose of propagating the belief in her original immunity.

This medal quickly grew famous by its miracles and drew crowds to the Rue du Bac, but the chapel was too small to hold them, and, furthermore, this constant running to and fro would have broken up the concentrated hours of the cloister. The Virgin arranged everything for the best. Just when she was appearing in the chapel M. Dufriche-Desgenettes was the rector of St Francis Xavier's, the church of the parish in which the Sisters' house was situated. He knew the alluring ventures suggested by the miraculous medal and was busy in disseminating it when he was nominated to be the rector of Notre-Dame des Victoires.

This district was one of the worst in the city; the church was empty from morning to night. After trying in vain to gather together a few of the faithful, he grew discouraged, and, further influenced thereto by his scruples, resolved to retire, thinking that another would succeed better perhaps than himself in pulling penitents out of that fish-pond of dead consciences. He was unusually obsessed with this notion when, on December 3, 1836, the morning of the feast of St Francis Xavier, the patron-saint of his former parish, he ascended the altar-steps to say Mass. He was so cruelly tortured by the obsession of having to leave everything that he could not collect his thoughts. However, he succeeded in pulling himself together just before the *Sanctus* and implored the Lord to deliver him from his torments. No sooner had he finished this prayer than he heard an interior voice saying distinctly: "Consecrate your parish to the most holy Immaculate Heart of Mary"; and at once he regained his inward calm. After Mass, he wonders whether he has been duped by an illusion, but the same words are repeated still more plainly. He returns home, and at one stroke writes, as if under dictation, the rule for a confraternity which is more especially to honour the Immaculate Conception, and, even before his plans were revealed in public, no one knows why or how, the deserted church is filled. Cures and conversions of all kinds take place in it. Notre-Dame des Victoires by degrees became the great pilgrimage of the Virgin in Paris.

Mary has crossed the river and fixed her domicile in the most tainted spot in the city, close to the Bourse, in the very core of the Jewry of banks and textiles. The devotion which arose in the Rue du Bac where she appeared has been transferred to the old church of the Augustinians, and the multitude of visitors who throng it every year is immense.

The hyperdulia peculiar to Lourdes is a replica, enlarged and put within reach of the whole world, of the devotion of Notre-Dame des Victoires, which is confined to the diocese of Paris. It is derived from that devotion and issues out of it, but the Virgin only called it into being after the old belief of the mother-churches of Paris had been imposed on the world by a pope.

Lastly, besides the two lines, regional and Parisian, which we have just explained, we may also, though the conditions of the connection are different, bring together the apparitions of Lourdes and those of La Salette. If it has no Parisian ancestry, the sanctuary of La Salette has a local derivation similar to that of Lourdes, for it, too, was born in a place ringed round with old pilgrim chapels more or less dead, and it has the peculiarity of being situated in a mountainous country like that of Lourdes.

Sixteen years after the apparition in the Rue du Bac and twelve years before those of Lourdes, at La Salette, near Corps in the Dauphiné, on the heights of the Alps, Mary spoke to little Melanie, and a spring gushed forth which became a vehicle for cures, just as did the one which later on wrought the same effects in the Pyrenees.

Only this time the Madonna never said a single word of the exemption of her Conception from impurity, but she wept and threatened, scourged the sins of priests and cloisters more particularly, and demanded a timely penance in expiation of all sorts of profligacy.

At the outset the pilgrimage had a wonderful vogue, then the difficulty of the communications, the impossibility of hauling up the sick and infirm by the badly marked zigzags on the mountain slopes, discouraged and diminished the numbers of the caravans of our Lady's clients. Furthermore, the common people of the district, largely made up of infidels and freemasons, who exploited the pilgrims and made fun of them, no doubt contributed their share to the more and more marked desertion of the crowds.

In short, while spiritual favours continued to be perceptibly bestowed, the pilgrimage fell away more and more, and scarcely included anyone except excursionists and folks of the neighbourhood when the Lourdes apparitions gave it the death-blow.

The Virgin quitted the Alps for the Pyrenees. And there, not on the top of the peak but at the foot of a mountain, in a grotto, as if She meant to come closer and to put herself at the disposal of all mankind, she appeared smiling as a glorious Virgin, and distributed her favours with both hands more generously than she had done before in her dispensaries on the Seine and in Dauphiné.

What had taken place in the twelve years' interval between the manifestations in the Alps and those in the Pyrenees? The Virgin repeats once more at Lourdes that it is fitting to do penance and to pray, but she ceases weeping, and utters no further rebukes nor threats.

It looks as if her Son's anger were appeased—and yet, during the interim, so far as can be judged, the lives of men had but gone from bad to worse; why, then, was there such a change of attitude, why this sudden outpouring of mercy?

There could be no explanation of it, did we not know that, even in addition to a few religious Orders which have not slackened in their penances, there are still to be found among the laity, especially among women, numbers who were stirred to make reparation by the sharp complaints of La Salette. Doubtless many made the sacrifice of self and restored the equilibrium which had been upset, and thus by their sufferings turned catastrophes aside.

We are in the dark; we feel dimly within us and above us conflicts perpetually breaking out afresh and coming to an end. There are three who take part in the match—God, the devil, and man; but one of the three, man, does not know how the game will end, though he is himself the stake in it.

If we now sum up these few remarks, we can establish this, that the Virgin's itinerary in France during the nineteenth century started from Paris, and, after a station at La Salette in the Alps, came to an end at Lourdes in the Pyrenees.

We may also note that the Mother of Christ chose as her residence such places as She had formerly occupied, resuscitating rather than creating in our own times such devotions as She drew from their own districts to propagate throughout the world.

We have already told how La Salette and Lourdes appear in the districts She had already inhabited. As for Paris, it is right to observe that in the Middle Ages

Saint-Séverin was already a living centre for pilgrimages; and we may also acknowledge that, apart from the reasons that induced the Virgin to use a Sister of St Vincent de Paul as her interpreter, She chose the Rue du Bac because, in that quarter on the left bank of the river, the devotion claimed to take its rise; and there it was very much alive just in those later ages when it was dying out in its seat at Saint-Séverin, invaded by the followers of Jansenius, and now become a chapel of ease to the cemetery of Saint-Médard, with its convulsionaries who came to pray at the tomb of the Abbé Desanguins, the confessor of Paris the deacon, who was buried in that church.

In the Rue du Bac, which was a nursery for communities in the seventeenth century, there was one, indeed, a few paces from the convent of the Grey Sisters at the corner of the Rue de Varennes. This was the monastery of the Recollettes, called the daughters of the Immaculate Conception, which was suppressed in 1792 and was specially intended to honour that prerogative of the Blessed Virgin.

Let us add that, when She crossed the bridges and installed herself on the right bank of the Seine, She betook herself to an ancient church which She had long known, and it belonged to her more particularly than did any other, for it had been devoted to her in the name of France by King Louis XIII, and baptised by him, on the capture of La Rochelle from the Huguenots, with the name of Notre-Dame des Victoires.

In Paris, as at La Salette and at Lourdes, she made use of country girls as her intermediaries, humble, rough and dull-witted folk. At La Salette and at Lourdes she spoke to shepherdesses, to Melanie and Bernadette, as She had formerly spoken to Liloye and to Anglèse of Sagazan; and in Paris where shepherdesses are lacking, She fixed her choice upon an old farm-servant who had become a Sister of Charity. Further let us note with regard to this that She did not look for her interpreter among the nuns of an Order of contemplatives, but among the religious of an active Order, founded at the very time of the building of Notre-Dame des Victoires And may we not to some extent presume that, because of this old simultaneity of origin and the sudden connexion in recent times of these two sanctuaries which the Virgin has exchanged for one another, some mysterious bond links this church with this Order?

Lastly, at La Salette, as at Lourdes, as well as formerly in Paris, at Saint-Séverin and in the Pyrenees, at Bétharram and at Garaison, She willed water to be the instrument of cures.

This question of the connexion of water with the Virgin has been very ingeniously treated by the Catholic occultist, M. Grillott de Givry in his stimulating book—*Les villes initiatiques, Lourdes.*

Truth to tell, the old symbolism of the Middle Ages was much concerned with this element, but did not regard it as a peculiar and unique emblem of the Virgin, and still less did it designate water as "the vital feminine principle in nature" which M. de Givry talks about.

It is quite clear that the comparison of the first chapter of Genesis with the first chapter of St Luke could not be avoided, and that hence arose the temptation of likening to one another the two operations of the Holy Ghost; first, in the days of creation brooding on the waters and overshadowing them in a manner, and then hovering, too, over the Virgin who is overshadowed by the Most High.

Water may, then, be one of the special emblems of the Virgin, but it is none the less quite true that more often, and almost always, indeed, symbolism attached a very different signification thereto, whether we are dealing with water properly so called, with sea or river, with spring or well.

According to this symbolism, water represents in various degrees Christ, the angels, Gospel teaching, baptism, charity, or the science of the saints; and, if we turn to the other side of its system of analogy, if we take it in its bad sense, water is a symbol of temptation, of the floods of sin, and of self-indulgence.

But if we confine ourselves to the best-known mode of interpretation, according to the writings of St Gregory the Great, of Rabanus Maurus, and of Peter of Capua, we find that water is, above all, the symbol of the Holy Spirit.

Moreover, it would be wiser to recognise this form of healing as only one of those used at will by the Virgin, for she often does without it. In such places as she causes springs to gush forth, at Lourdes, for instance, she heals the sick and infirm completely without their having any need of drinking the water of the spring or of bathing in the piscinas.

After all, water is but a material sign of regeneration. After curing the soul of the consequences of the fall, it may heal the bodies whose sufferings are its results. Such, perhaps, is the reason why the Virgin makes use of this special procedure, recalling the sacrament of baptism.

On some occasions, she makes this element an aid in the bestowal of her favours, and we know not why, sets it aside on others.

The springs of La Salette and Lourdes were prefigured in any case in the Old Testament by the Jordan, which set free Naaman the Syrian; in the New by the miracle of the pond, called Probatica which was stirred by an angel.

II

IF anyone was never stirred with the desire to go to
Lourdes, that man was myself. To begin with, I have
no liking for crowds streaming in processions, bawling hymns, and I agree with St John of the Cross in
his *Ascent of Mount Carmel:* "I strongly approve of the
man," he writes, "who goes on pilgrimage outside the
set times, in order to escape joining up with the pilgrim
crowd. When throngs swarm in, I recommend him to
have nothing to do with them. He always runs the risk
of returning from them more distraught than when he
started."

Next, I am not anxious to see miracles. I know quite
well that the Virgin can perform them at Lourdes or
anywhere else. My faith does not rest on my own reason nor upon any degree of the certainty of my own
sense-perceptions; it depends upon an inner sense of
assurance derived from inward evidences; with all deference to the pundits of psychiatry and the knowing
pedagogues, who cannot explain anything and label the
phenomena of the supernatural life of which they are
ignorant as autosuggestion or derangement, mysticism

is a fearlessly exact science; I have been able to verify a certain number of its results, and that is all I ask for in order to believe: it is enough for me.

And now, while awaiting the arrival of the great international pilgrimages, here am I, for the second time, owing to circumstances distantly connected with one another and almost altogether involuntary, already installed for some weeks past in this town. This morning it is raining, as it does rain in this country—that is to say, in buckets; and, as I sit near the cottage window where I am living at the top of the rise on the road to Pau, I look at the panorama of Lourdes through my window-pane streaming with tears of rain.

The background is closely curtailed and compressed together by the mountains, between which rise bunches of white steam, while higher up race along dark smoky clouds and sooty tufts roll away, as if from factory chimneys. The top of one of these heights appears to be smoking, whilst the peak of another is clear of clouds and seems extinct; here and there, scarves of grey wadding girdle the pass of the lowest hills and straggle loosely downwards; as for the summits whitened with perpetual snow, they are now utterly lost in fog; the Great Gers and Little Gers, the two nearest mountains, look, through the reeking mist, like immense pyramids of clinkers, huge cinder-heaps.

Oh, the sadness of this sky streaked across with fine threads of rain! At the bottom of yonder range of hills, just before me, the Gave, a torrent rushing on day and night, boils and bubbles over chunks of rock, and, before expanding farther on into a peaceful river, girdles with foam a building surmounted by a pointed belfry and surrounded with a lean garden planted with firs and poplars. You might take the building for a reformatory, loopholed as are its stiff straight walls, right at the top, with most diminutive garret windows; it is the Convent of the Poor Clares. To the left a bridge bestrides the river and joins the new town of Lourdes, the houses of which I can see, with the old town dominated by an ancient keep which looks as if it were made for stage-scenery, with side-wings of painted canvas; anyone might take it for an imitation. Lastly, to the right are the Esplanade and its trees leading to the Rosary[1] and to the double rising terrace overhung by the Basilica, the outline of which stands out, all white, against the slope of the Espelugues, on which, amidst clearings encircled with greenery, to mark the Stations of Calvary, arise huge crosses.

And behind the Esplanade and its lawns, below the balustraded terraces, two gasometers, one coated with a kind of water-green ripolin, the other painted with the yellow ochre of a public convenience, bulge forth, horrible to see; these sheet-iron pies cover, in one case, a panorama of Jerusalem; in the other, a panorama of Lourdes.

All this is not very captivating from an artistic point of view, and the cathedral, perched aloft in the air on a narrow ledge of rock, is no better. Flimsy and scrimpy, without any ornamentation of worth, it calls forth

---

1 "The Rosary" with a capital initial is used throughout for "the Church of the Rosary" at Lourdes.

wretched memories of the cork models of churches used for window-dressing in certain trades; it takes its cue from the aesthetics of cork-merchants: the least of village chapels erected in the Middle Ages, compared with such contraband Gothic, looks like a masterpiece of delicacy and strength; the best feature, despite its coldness and bareness, would be the double stone-built terrace which leads from the level of the Esplanade up to the great doors, if it were not spoilt at the culminating point by the frightful roof of the Rosary, bulging out beneath the base of the Basilica—a roof shaped on the colossal mould of a Savoy cake, flanked with three domed boiler-covers, made of zinc.

Seen sideways from where I am, this rotunda, with its double sloping terrace undulating downwards from the roof to the ground, looks like an enormous crab extending its long pincers towards the old town. And below the terrace, under the Basilica and along by the Rosary, fronting the bed of the Gave, runs a broad walk before the piscinas and the Grotto, and then stops, abruptly barred by a hill on the face of which is marked a zigzag in the form of an M. It climbs, a footpath bordered with trees, behind the Basilica and leads to the house belonging to the Fathers of the Grotto and to the episcopal residence built a little way from the top.

All this looks lank and lean, sorry and stunted, for the broad spaciousness of the mountains is too close and crushing for it; but the ready-made scenery vanishes when we see the fiery hollow in the rock beneath the Basilica itself, a flaming cave burning under its side: there lies the interest of Lourdes.

The Grotto! Take away the futile statue set up in the embrasure in which the Virgin appeared, and you begin to soar freely. You think of the heap of prayers you undertook before leaving Paris, and you offer them to her one by one as well as you can; everyone has to beg for the cure or conversion of friends or relations, and everyone unpacks in Her presence the poor parcel of bodily suffering or moral misery he has brought with him. There is a great silence; all are kneeling and lost in recollection; now that the Grotto is again accessible we hasten to obtain from the Madonna such favours as we want. We have her to ourselves just for a few hours more. Tomorrow the pilgrimages, which have arrived during the night, will fill the Grotto to overflowing and there will be no possibility of getting into it, or even of becoming recollected on the seats ranged before her, for there will be the ceaseless noise of the hymns and sermons.

So will it be with the unseen spring, the water of which flows through the twelve brass taps from a fountain made to the left of it. We shall have to form queues if we want to fill a can or empty a glass.

Already people are hurrying to drink there; they are handing tin mugs to and fro; some of them toss them off at a draught, others swallow only half, and pour the rest over their hands, and rub their faces and bathe their ears and eyes with it. Women gather up their dresses and tuck them between their knees so as not to wet them, and they scold the children who splash themselves by shaking bottles which are too full; everyone takes precautions as if the town were about to be besieged.

While awaiting the predicted mass-attack of the crowds, the charm of Lourdes, now intimate and familiar, without hustle and hubbub, works; you relish the agreeableness of a town induced by its love of gain to lay itself out to please, and feel a fraternal friendliness towards all whose thoughts are in tune with your own, and who, like yourself, are lying in wait for the Virgin's blessings. At last you get to know, without trying to find out, why one man walks in this direction and why that woman is there, and you become interested in their cure or in the result of their plans. There is something of the comradeship of a bivouac in such a gathering of people encamped in a country town; for you cannot take a few steps anywhere without meeting one another. You pass each other on the Esplanade, find yourselves side by side in the Basilica and its Crypt, or rub elbows in the Rosary of the Grotto, and you almost want to bow to each other without knowing one another.

In truth no one stays at home, and everybody lives out of doors, whether it rains or not. From morning till nightfall you follow the same track time after time, seeing nothing but the faces you have seen again and again, except the plaster statues of our Lady, with their eyes turned heavenwards, robed in white and wearing blue sashes; not a single shop is without its medals and candles and rosaries and scapulars and pamphlets full of miracles; both old and new Lourdes are crammed with them; even the hotels have them on sale; and that goes on in street after street for miles, starting from old Lourdes with the poor woman who hawks little rosaries with steel chains and crosses and huge characteristic

Lourdes rosaries of chocolate-coloured wood made at Bétharram, sold at threepence apiece, and harshly tinted chromos of Bernadette kneeling taper in hand at the Virgin's feet, and Lilliputian statues and medals like dolls' money minted by the gross from odds and ends of brass: and all these things grow better and bigger and larger as you get nearer the new town; the statues swarm increasingly and end by becoming, not less ugly, but enormous. The chromos broaden out, disguising Soubirous' daughter as a lady's maid; the medals' stamp is enlarged and their metal changed; gold and silver appear, and, when you come to the avenue of the Grotto, there is a regular outburst of gewgaws *de luxe!* No longer do the rosaries hang up in bunches outside, but they recline in glass cases on beds of rose-tinted velvet padding; the beads are now made of lapis lazuli, coral and amethysts, gold or silver-mounted, and stationers' knickknacks, pencil-cases, penholders, paperweights of various Pyrenean marbles mingle with them, reinforced by Paris-made wares and jewellery from the Palais Royal, hallowed by the attachment of a cross or a medal.

And then begins a frantic competition; you are hooked in at every step by the shops all over the town; and you go to and fro and turn this way and that amidst the tumult, but always end up, whatever road you take, at the Grotto. This Grotto, of irregular shape, fairly high at the threshold, not quite so high farther in and very low on one side, is decorated with all sorts of ex-votos, with blackened crutches fastened with wire to the arch above and dancing up and down at the least breath of wind, with a portable altar for episcopal Masses, and with a little wheeled hand-cart—a dust cart for the refuse of the votive candles.

To the left, near the fountain, is a square stone building used as a watchman's lodge and sacristy, and farther on is a shop where they sell devotional wares (*la bondieuserie*) and wax candles. To the right, almost right under the almond-shaped hole in which the Virgin appeared as in a frame, is a pulpit, here a fixture, which is filled during the pilgrimages by the missionaries or priests who aim, like catapults, the prayers of the faithful at the vaults of heaven to force them to pour down, as through the burst gates of a dam, torrents of grace.

Baked with burning tapers, carpeted like the bottom of a fireplace with soot perpetually warm and wet, the Grotto of Massabielle, with its ever-burning brazier, is strangely worth studying.

Near the entrance of the grille is a crown of brass candle-stands, provided with great flat plates, bristling with points on which the wax-candles are impaled and burn. At the bottom of the Grotto, level with the ground, all along the rock, stretch three black iron strips in rows; they are pierced with rings, in which are set candle-boxes; the lower and the larger ones are, in reality, not so much rings as funnels, which they vaguely resemble; they are specially used to embrace enormous wax candles costing over sixty francs each and lasting for weeks; then come triangular stands let into the stone, and spikes are stuck in, here and there, near hollows covered with nets, in which people put letters, collected in too human a fashion, for our Lady.

And all these candles sputter and burn each other away, varying according to their height and price; the smallest tapers sink down molten about a wick which bulges out into a mushroom, changing from cherry-red to black; larger ones waste away more slowly in streamlets of rice-water, which gradually congeal into white pools of fat; others become striated and rugose, and, with their worm-eaten furrows and bony protuberances, resemble the corrugated bark of elm trees; others, again, seem to sprout upwards above their wicks and burn away like night-lights in the bottom of a glass covered with lacework round the edges and festooned with ramifications like lace-edged devotional pictures. Some, too, are faded and very old, dotted, like noses, with pimples and hooks, dishonest tapers, deceiving the buyer and robbing God, tapers in which the stearine stem is enveloped in a layer of wax that weeps yellow tears while its centre melts into a vitreous wash surrounding the broiled peduncles of plain candles.

Here we find a sort of antipodes of Pentecost: the fiery tongues rise heavenwards and do not descend from on high; but they invoke the Holy Ghost in the very form of his own choice; they play the part of liturgical supplications, imploring our Lord in the very language used by his prototypes; and if one recalls the proper of the season of Pentecost, in which water is associated with fire, one grasps the mysterious alliance of the two elements of fire and water at Lourdes.

These fire-blossoms are cultivated by an old gardener living on the premises, who gets browned as he goes to and fro before the glowing hearth of the Grotto—a real gardener in a blue apron with pockets, smooth-shaven, with his gardener's tools, pruning-knife, rake, shovel, and a wheelbarrow as big as a little cart.

From morning to night, without haste, he tidies up for the Virgin, scraping the stalactites from the candle-holders and their spiked frames and stands, stirring up the ground saturated with a dressing of tallow and with a fine powder of snow, in which fiery flowers appear to grow of themselves and to spring from the pollen of sparks carried away in the smoke by puffs of wind; and he snuffs the cotton pistils of these flowers, cleans their stalks, picks off the white worms of their drop-pings, unearths their dying trunks, and throws them to be consumed in one of the basins where they finally perish in flaming stumps, for here everything is burnt up honestly, quite to the contrary of what happens in other churches, in which the candle-women blow out the half-burnt tapers to sell them again.

Then he takes a fistful of little tapers, like a bunch of asparagus, and lights them all together at one stroke and thrusts them into one of the rings of the row at the back as soon as the great wax candle in the iron mug is dead. The wax-lights swarm in increasing numbers. There are whole cartfuls waiting for their turn to be unloaded, and he sorts out these white rods, separates them from one another or gathers them into bundles, sticks together those with broken stumps by warming them, watches the lighting without a moment's rest, and transplants this or that taper which is hanging fire and languishing to a better situation, less sheltered from the fresh air: and still the work ever begins anew, for as fast as tapers go out, others arise.

This trousered Vestal is also a Danaid in breeches, for the Grotto is a bottomless well of fire; from the provinces, from abroad, and from all parts of the world, every morning orders flow in, and the question is, how to finish up the day's supplies without being overwhelmed with the fresh arrivals of tomorrow; and whatever is done the heaps grow into piles; here you might set up a wax-candle factory just as you might start a wood-yard anywhere else. All the people sell wax-lights, or rather sham wax candles, for they retail as wax "from the bee," despite all liturgical regulations, nothing but rolls of old tallow treated with sulphuric acid to refine and harden them.

But such subterfuges as these, inevitably due to the constantly increasing allurement of the sales, disappear in the dazzling light of the brazier which devours both paraffin and wax with indifference, and, looking at these hedges of fiery prayers, calls to mind the symbolism of the wax-candle as set forth by Peter Esquilinus and St Ambrose.

The wax-light is made of three things: wax—for the most spotless flesh of Christ; the wick inserted therein—for his most pure soul hidden beneath the covering of his body; and fire—for the emblem of his divinity.

Thus the candle is a figure of Christ; and hence it is brought to the Virgin that she may herself offer the Father his own Son to intercede for us; but it must be owned that worship, under the form of *dulia*, as practiced in most churches, is absurd. We offer candles, quite properly, to certain saints as private gifts for themselves; and thus we honour them with a personal offering to the point of getting prayers addressed to them by your Lord instead of getting them to address the prayers to our Lord, which is nonsense.

Unless we accept the mediocre symbolism of St Charles Borromeo, who took the candle to be an emblem of the three theological virtues, and compared its light to Faith, its form to Hope, and its heat to Charity.

In that, however, we should light them before a statue of one of the denizens of heaven to obtain his helm in getting our Lord to increase in us the working of those virtues which rise, so hindered by the leg of our sins, with such tardiness and trouble.

At Lourdes, however, another and a more lively and far-reaching symbolism is imperative—the symbolism of the communion of souls, which is so transparently signified by the mingling of their lights. Indeed, if one thinks of it, the spectacle of these thousands of burning candles is wonderful!

What wild rendings of heart and what trembling hopes they reveal! How many infirmities, sicknesses, domestic distresses, desperate supplications, conversions, and maddening terrors do they stand for! This Grotto is the shelter and refuge of all racked with the anxieties of this world, the refuge to which all the crushed in life fly for protection and where they are stranded in the end; it is the last resort of the condemned, and of afflictions that nothing can alleviate: all the suffering of the world is condensed into this narrow space.

See how the candles weep the tears of mothers in despair, and perchance give an exact counterpart of the sorrows that consume them; some weep hurriedly, pouring down hot tears; others are more restrained, shedding slower drops; and all are faithful to the charge entrusted to them; all, before final extinction, writhe increasingly while their flames shoot up in a last cry to the Virgin!

Clearly, some are more eloquent than others in pleading with God; and there is no doubt that the humblest are the most persuasive; the pretentious columns of stearin, bought on the spot or sent by the wealthy, in virtue of the pomp they proclaim, have less chance, despite the greater length of their supplication, of favourable acceptance, and certainly the divine pity inclines towards the poor little tapers lighted in bundles, which mingle their yearnings and their lights together, and combine, as they do in church, in one common supplication. They are a true likeness of the poor and destitute who help one another, whilst the aristocratic candles live alone and apart.

Then it is that the lowly toil of the fireman at the Grotto is exalted and becomes sublime.

This man, thinking only of the cleaning of his spiked frames and stands, unconsciously forwards the magnificent work of the communion of souls. He gathers the prayers together and sets them up before our Lady in sheaves of fire; he turns the ordinary conditions of life upside down mingling one class with another; he brings them back to the teachings of the Gospels; he seconds, by amalgamating the roots of the big candles with the rootlets of the little ones which are ending in a molten flow, the entreaties of the rich by uniting them with those of the poor before the Lord, thus forcing the Virgin's hand in a way by increasing the too light weight of their prayers, saving the weaker ones with the help of the stronger.

Here we find Society turned upside down, the world inside out: the poor are the givers of alms to the rich.

The candle, which is looked upon by the unbeliever as one of the most puerile forms of superstition is one of the most extraordinary of agencies used by those whose feelings it embodies and for whose wishes it serves as a vehicle. Souls seem, indeed, to impregnate it with their own aura, and I imagine a transference of feeling to inanimate and inert things, on the analogy of Colonel de Rochas's experiments; I fancy—apart from any question of hypnotism in this case—that by the sole power of faith these stearin candles may be possibly injected with effluences, and thus retain somewhat of the feeling of those who offer them, and that they really pray.

We may also be allowed to suppose that the element of Fire at Lourdes is but the servant of the other element—*i.e.*, Water. Many cures take place at the spring or within the piscinas: people begin with the Grotto and end with the Spring. Lourdes may perhaps be summed up in these words: What you beseech with Fire, you obtain with Water.

III

THE time for the great international pilgrimages has come; the town is assailed from every quarter and goes giddy with excitement. Pilgrims from Lorraine, from Champagne, from Provence, from Normandy, and from the Rouergue and Berri are here. An army of Belgians, landed yesterday, invades the Esplanade and lines the streets; this morning we are expecting the trains from Brittany along with a fresh squadron of Belgians and Dutchmen.

Lourdes is already full to bursting within its indestructible belt of mountains. It has stopped raining; a sort of violet powder falls from the sky with an implacable purity on the mountain range, which begins to show up in outline. The Great and the Little Gers are gilding with the sunlight their cindery carapace of boulders, and a few clinging stretches of pasture bedaub their sides with dashes of green. Something is slowly ascending a furrow hollowed out in one of their slopes: it looks like a white worm creeping upwards; it is the funicular railway, climbing sometimes in open daylight, sometimes through dark tunnels, to the top.

The sun seems to be winnowing abroad well-being and sifting joy over the valley, through which resounds a hunting horn used to rouse attention by the ragman whose cart appears now on the road in the distance.

I go down to be present at the arrival of the faithful from Finisterre and Morbihan; the streets of the old town and the bridge are overflowing; you have to elbow your way through; the lazy flock of Bretons goes round and round on its own track, just marking time where it is, and is driven back by its priests, who harry it as if they were sheepdogs; but the shops full of pious trinkets hypnotise the women, and they have to be dragged away by the arm or pushed in the back to get them to move on. Half awake and bewildered, they gaze as if they were coming out of a dream, dragging along with them huge baskets and cans, and most of them walk arm-in-arm, scarcely speaking, with minds benumbed, ruminating, like cattle, on what none can tell. The fact is that they are utterly knocked up by the long nights in the train, and feel quite adrift. In any case, they impart a dash of colour to the monotonous greys and blacks of the crowd drawn from other provinces. The men have stuck to their velvet ribboned hats, their vests and waistcoats of royal blue or episcopal violet, laced with canary-yellow embroideries and dotted with buttons like little brass bells; but only from the waist upwards have they retained the tints and fashions of their native soil; underneath, they are just like anyone else, of a squalid ugliness which clashes with the apparent newness up above. A zouave's belt, blue as the blue of a washerwoman, defines the respective zones of the curious vest and of the annoying breeches, picked up amongst the ready-for-cash reach-me-downs of a seaport town. Some of them have flaps, but like the more recent ones, they are woven of pea-soup-tinted or slaty wools; a few even have turned to a heavy brown hue through getting soiled and shiny from constant wear; in the whole pilgrimage only one man shows himself in full costume with galligaskins and leggings coloured cinnamon—an old fellow, broad and tall and upright, with long white hair, a rosy complexion, and withered eyes shrinking back into dark, deep, shrivelled hollows.

And almost all these sailors have set features, skins like old boxwood, and clear cold blue pupils like those of the black sheep of Finisterre.

The women are stout and bony, with skins like onion-peel, salted with spray, eyes of lapis lazuli or sea-green; and the young girls, with their bird-like heads and hard skulls, are bound up in petticoats with bell-shaped flounces purfled in acid hues of rose and loud colours of aniline violets. These, too, are from anywhere from the waist downwards, and become true Breton women from thence upwards as far as the back of their necks; some are accoutred with goffered collars fluted in little tucks of the period of Louis XIII, and their bodies braided with half-moons and crab-claws of velvet; one or two from the depths of Finisterre are like Dutchwomen, with their orange valanced gowns and the spangled embroideries of their headgear; and all are recognisable in the crowd by their queer and many-shaped bonnets; indeed, they affect the strangest forms, from that of a flower pot set upside down on their chignons, from starched helmets and stunted mitres, to butterflies' wings and lady-slippers' flap-eared pockets.

In this pack from Armorica which worms its way through the streets and over the bridge, cripples and maimed people, deformed children with stunted limbs, old men with huge pear-shaped goitres, old women hobbling on T-shaped crutches, blind folk with pupils like the white of an egg, are surrounded and supervised by the Sisters of the Holy Ghost, whose habit is apparently made of unbleached canvas, with just a touch of black at the tip of their hoods, and tinges with a fleeting smile of whiteness the sombre darkness of clothes and dresses. The priests, with the features of farmers or fishermen, get impatient at being unable to hasten the progress of their flock, but their efforts at remonstrance are in vain; the women are mirthful, and one of them stops in the middle of the bridge on the footway to have her boots cleaned, and has a dispute with the bootblack, who asks her to pay a penny; for she says she only owes him a halfpenny because her feet are small.

At last the procession reaches a bronze statue of St Michael waltzing round in an ungainly fashion upon the prostrate body of something like a lawyer disguised as a devil, and passes by the Calvary standing at the beginning of the Esplanade—an offering by this same Brittany to our Lady of Lourdes. The priest at the head of the cortege halts and turns back, and the herd follows his example; he raises his arm and the hymn begins, while the procession goes on:

"We come once more from far Armor,
Where earth is hard and hearts are brave.
Proud of the Faith, nought else we crave.
We come once more from far Armor."[1]

And all turn their steps towards the Grotto, cleaving asunder the multitudes of pilgrims from all quarters who are distinguished from one another by their badges, for here everyone wears a ribbon or a rosette, everyone is decorated! The Belgians have, in their buttonholes, little tiny cockades—black, yellow, and red, the colours of their national flag; the men of Burgundy have the same colours with a metal cross on it; the Normans a red flannel cross; the Bretons a Sacred Heart, also made of red flannel; the people of the Berri a white daisy on a background of ashy blue; and how many more are there!

Driven hither and thither by the eddies of the crowd, tugged forward and thrust back into queues by the Sisters of the Holy Ghost and the clergy, the Bretons, nevertheless, reach the Grotto, but it is quite full. All along the river people are swarming, and the space between the grille of the Grotto and the parapet by the Gave is very restricted. The stretcher-bearers, whose business it is to keep order, stand opposite one another and stretch ropes to secure a free road for the conveyances and chairs bringing the sick from the hospital. At this time the Basilica, the crypt upon which it is built, and the Rosary are crammed to overflowing;

---

1 "Armor," from "ar" = on, and" "mor" = sca, means the seaside, *i.e.* Armorica, roughly the peninsula of Brittany.

groups are standing at the doors, thrown wide-open, and hear the Mass a distance; and now the Espelugues hill, up which runs the Way of the Cross, comes to life, and, like a slowly revolving spiral, breaks forth into hymns.

It appears to be on the move with those who are climbing the zigzag paths on its slopes: this is a pilgrimage from Quercy, winding, with a banner ahead of it, and shouting, with voices like the banging of sheets of corrugated iron, a hymn in which one catches such sounds as "De Dious la rouzado" and "pitchoun."[1]

I know these fellows: they might be called the coal-heavers of Lourdes; they are all black—clothes, caps, and coats; not even a spot of white linen about their necks; and their very features seem to be thrown into relief with dabs of charcoal. Yesterday they were prowling and scowling in strings of pious jabberers through the streets of the town; and the shopkeepers, knowing they would buy nothing, were jeering as they listened to their jargon as they hung around their wares.

And while these sombre Southerners wend their way, vociferating, up the zigzag paths on the hillside, others have succeeded by hook or by crook in massing together the Bretons near the Grotto, and they are now listening to the sermon of one of their rectors perched up in the pulpit. They are standing uncovered and all attention, and, while running through the rosary, they all fasten their blissful gaze upon the white and blue statue of our Lady. They are bustled and hustled, and their huge feet are stamped upon to open a way through

---

1 *La rosée de Dieu* and *petit* in French.

their ranks for the bedridden sick, but no one protests or stops praying; they are no longer the sleepy louts of a few hours ago, but good and humble people, full of the simple and strong piety of their race, invoking the Virgin whom they have come so far to venerate. After the rosary, very quietly, led by the Sisters, they file off, two by two, into the Grotto, and kiss the rock, entering the grille by one gate and leaving it by the other, and then they will go, in single file, to drink of the spring.

I betake myself to the piscinas. Confined within railings and closed by ropes across the entrance, the space before the three dwarf muddled Gothic buildings, stuck in at the bottom of the rock beneath the side of the Basilica, only a few paces from the Grotto, is filled with the conveyances of the sick; and stretcher-bearers in *bérets*, with leather braces, which are the free passes and sesames of Lourdes, raise the pillow of a sick man to let him drink from a tin mug, and very devoted they are to the unfortunates, whom they draw from the hospital to the piscinas, acting as beasts of burden.

A priest who looks like a jailbird, with five days' growth of beard, from some out-of-the-way hole in the depths of the provinces, flings himself upon his knees, with his arms outstretched in the form of a cross, right in front of everyone. He says the rosary in a loud voice, invokes the Virgin with great cries, and implores her to heal the patients who are being bathed; and his kindled soul lights up his features, and, little by little, works upon the onlookers till they are inflamed. How well he prays, poor country curate that he is! With what a voice, and with what eyes!—eyes of both fire and water, firebrands flashing into tears!

And still the ambulances come in, full of wan paralytics with relaxed lips, inspecting one wonders what on the ground; of the dropsied, with heads thrown back as if in aversion from the haunting panic of stomachs swollen like the bulge of an oil-bottle; of consumptives, sunken and sad, whose glazed eyes wander round; and of the heart-diseased, choking and lifting their necks into the air in their efforts to breathe more freely.

And the ambulances are drawn close together, and now comes the charabanc of the serious cases lying out at full length on mattresses placed on litters: livid men and women with distorted features, pinched noses, mouths like two lines of ashes, and poached eyes in a ring of lilac amidst something white.

The stretcher-bearers hasten to take down the litters carefully and put them near the doors of the piscinas, which are closed with curtains.

In the presence of these pictures of sorrow which are passing by, the kneeling priest whips up the crowd and excites its feelings with the pitiful cries of his broken voice:

"Lord, save our sick!"

And the furious thunder of the *Aves* starts again:

"Mary, we love thee."

And the rumbling of the *Aves* redoubles—and the doorways of the piscinas open. People lean forward eagerly to make out the faces of those who are being carried out; they are expecting a cure, and they find bedridden creatures still living to suffer; alas! for these our supplications of this morning have been in vain. Well, let us look inside and see if, in default of any complete cure, there may not be some alleviation or amelioration. I cross the ambulance-yard and draw aside the bath-room curtain.

The first time I entered into these rooms I met with a surprise; after Zola's narrative, I thought that they must be very large, for he always filled his canvasses as if he were a scene-painter; I supposed there were at least three airy and commodious apartments, with great baths sunk in them, around which the bathers and the sick would be carrying on their exercises with ease. There is nothing of the kind: the rooms are just about the size of cheap cabins for bathers. In place of a door there was a curtain; then three walls: the one at the bottom provided with glazing which gave no light, and on it was painted a figure of the Virgin, and beneath it was a small statue of Our Lady of Lourdes; the two others are plain and unadorned partitions; lastly, in the middle there is sunk a shallow stone bath, into which you descend by a few steps, and the furniture consists of a single chair. It is in this dim chamber that the Virgin, turned into a bath-attendant, works; it is in this damp den, and with this putrid water, that she operates.

And you are seized with distress; you almost tremble, withdrawing suddenly within yourself, when you reflect that she keeps unseen in this narrow room, that you are perhaps brushing against her, and that in a moment, if she will, she may prove her presence by a cure!

You feel you ought to have Bernadette's white soul to dare to stay so close to her unabashed. You feel yourself so small, and, indeed, rather ashamed of walking about there as a curious inquirer; but, after all, you doubtless have your uses, since you have come to pray for the sick, and are speaking to her, not of yourself, but of them.

And you look for her in a mechanical way, and all you see is her poor effigy painted on a windowpane or modelled in plaster. You look into the water, which might reflect her smile if it had not lost the power of reflecting any sort of likeness after being muddied with the bathing of many wounds; it is opaque and dead; and nevertheless it is alive, and, ever since the apparitions, ready to obey the orders of Prophet and Psalmist who bade it, long before her Son was born, celebrate his praises; and it does so by proclaiming his miracles now that it has been chosen by his Mother as a vehicle of healing.

This morning the narrow corridor, leading to the antechamber for disrobing and to the bathers' rooms, is blocked up with occupied stretchers at the time of my arrival. An old gentleman, with a head like an egg, bald on top and hairy down below, is rushing about in a cyclist's get-up. He gives orders with an offhand swagger, lectures the bathers, writes down the number of baths in a pocket-book with an important air, and acts the part of the big fly on the wheel in a style to make one laugh, were it not for the sadness of the sight before one's eyes.

Now they are doing their utmost to undress a sick man whose back is one great sore; a horrible corpse-like smell of pus takes you by the throat; the man is torn in twain and groans with his mouth wide open, exposing his teeth. For modesty's sake, they fasten a waist-cloth round him; a belt is slipped under his loins, and, with all the adroitness they can muster, the four bath-attendants let him down into the piscina. On coming into contact with the chilly water, all his skin seems to ripple over his body in waves; he suffocates, with his head thrown back upon his shoulders; they pull him out, and, without wiping him dry, put on his clothes and carry him off.

All this time one has done one's best to pray; but how can anyone get beyond labial prayer, how think of what one is saying? The patient has half swooned away and does not know where he is, and the sick attendants are engrossed in their hard and trying work; and I, while I beg for the cure of this poor man, am distracted by the sight before me; so the only thing to reckon upon as of any real use must be the more unhampered supplications outside, which I can hear going on with vehemence as soon as the curtain is drawn up.

And it falls again upon a new litter which is being brought in. From it emerges a being who is bent double, whose face is haggard with suffering and leaves me utterly upset. Oh, the pity of it! His wrappings are taken off and his flannel waistcoat; he is a skeleton streaming with perspiration. They let him down gently into the water; he clenches it in his fists and his throat rattles. He is taken out and put back on his stretcher, still wet—and now comes another.

What a look is his! Two gas-jets lighted in the eye-sockets of a death's head, and yet raised in hope or cast down in fear. They strip him of his shirt; it is flecked, here and there, with spots of gum and of fresh blood, and stiffened elsewhere with marks of dry humour which make it look like a sticking plaster. And the man displays great pomegranate like hollows in his sides.

As soon as he is in the water, he pants hoarsely, with his eyes staring out of his head, and wads of lint which had not been removed float about. They take him out, and, after dipping them in the piscina, they plaster his linen dressings on him somehow or other; and a young priest, lying on a mattress, fully dressed, comes next. He is dying of some kind of heart-disease in its last stage. They unbutton his cassock and take off his shirt, and, on the order of the gentleman who registers the baths in his pocketbook, only a few lotions are applied to his chest.

The bearers return once more. Fearful screams break out-the cries of a child begging not to be put into the bath!

I go into the other bath-room: the same sights meet my eyes. The sick are lying on stretches while the water is still moving and lapping against the walls of the bathing place. From time to time whiffs of iodoform impregnate the atmosphere infected by the bitter breath and the wounds of the diseased; everywhere scraps of lint and wads stained with matter and blood, are trailing about.

The water has turned into a hideous broth, a sort of grey slops with bubbles in it, and red bladders and whitish blisters swim round in this molten gin into which they keep on plunging people.

Here is the perpetual miracle of Lourdes; the Sick are flung into contaminated excipients without waiting for the digestion of what they have eaten; women are plunged in up to the neck just when the most rudimentary common sense forbids any woman to take a bath—often, in such cases, turning the water into a pool of purple—and no congestion ensues; nor are they affected by the shock of the chill icy water, nor by being left unwiped. Antiseptic dressings, made so much of in surgery, are here simply replaced by compresses of Lourdes water, and sores are none the worse for it. Never were such slights inflicted upon hygiene and never was medical science so flouted. Yet here neither occurs infection, nor is any disease aggravated, even if it be not cured; and such exemption also extends to the hospital, in which the bedridden hardly ever die, although they have been worn out by the fatigue of the journey and arrive in an almost dying condition. Indeed, deaths are very rare in this institution at Lourdes. Taking an average of four days and a thousand cases, which in other hospitals would give a mortality of twenty at least, we find here—and that for the last twenty years—the fatalities, in the same conditions, number one or two.

If you have no belief in divine intervention, how can you explain such an assured impunity as is only to be found at Lourdes, and as long as you remain within the zone protected by the Virgin?

IV

THE new hospital of Notre-Dame des Sept Douleurs is a huge unfinished building. Such as it is, it manages to harbour the multitude of patients that crowd into it. They sleep on all sides, even in the rooms lately begun, separated from the open-air by mere wooden partitions. And they also eat everywhere, even in the yards over which tarpaulins have been stretched, and in sheds in which a number of boards have been put upon trestles—and here is what is really extraordinary—amidst all the uproar of camp-life, amidst the influx and the reflux of the coming and going of sick cases arriving and departing with the pilgrimages to which they belong, in this constant promiscuity of people from every country, many of whom do not even understand French, there reign a friendly discipline and perfect order. The food is well cooked and punctually served; all who cannot feed themselves are helped; priests are at the beck and call of the bedridden who want to make their confessions; stretcher-bearers are ever ready to carry them to the Grotto and to bring them back; and, nevertheless, a few Sisters of

Saint-Frai, who are in charge of the kitchen and the re-
fectories, suffice for the work, with the help of the sick
attendants who have come by train and of the women
of the hospitality guild of Our Lady of Lourdes.

All this involves a very wise understanding of the
division of labour and of the distribution of hardship.
During the many years in which this work has been going on, all has been running smoothly; but it must also
be said that the sick who come to implore the Virgin
to heal them are devout and resigned and very amiable,
and that those who look after them do it out of charity,
and, if required, I believe they would put up with many
vexations and many complaints before committing any
sin of impatience. In any case, Lourdes is a cloak-room
for human failings: there they are left on arriving, and
no doubt they are fetched away again when people
leave, for nothing is more difficult than to set aside the
old man; but at least a provisional purification of souls
is wrought, over and above other graces scattered by the
Virgin, by contact with the gratitude of life's victims
and with the mercy of those who look after them.

The entrance of the hospital has no pomposity
about it. In the court before it, behind the railings that
cut it off from the street, is a bivouac of ambulances. At
the moment all have just come back from the Grotto,
and stretcher-bearers, broken with fatigue, now that
the patients have been taken to their beds, are lying at
full length in their places on the cushions and are talking, as they smoke, with others who are coming and
going, holding cups of soup or milk, under the arcades
along by the dreadful wards of the ground-floor, the

rooms of the dangerous cases in which is gathered up the surpassing horror of incurable diseases and of the agonizing who have been carried away to Lourdes in bad third-class compartments from every quarter of France and of other lands.

The ward on the right is reserved for women, and it wrecks your heart as soon as you enter it; it is crammed with beds packed closely together, and in them lie motionless women with their eyes closed, and yet not asleep, for they open them with a sudden scared look, and then shut them again. What haggard and bloodless faces! What a look of weariness of everything and of sickness of life, of hazy hope and of fear! And the wretchedness of their parcels, the poverty of their rags and cardboard packets, of their twopenny-halfpenny handbags, heaped up near the beds, adds pity for their material distress to one's compassion for these poor creatures.

Here, one raises herself suddenly, and, seized with hiccups, throws up mouthfuls of blood, while a lady runs to support her and wipes her lips with a napkin; there, another utters a short cry in a hoarse voice and writhes while they hurry round her and moisten her temples, making her inhale smelling-salts, and assuring her that her torments will soon be over and that the Virgin will cure her.

In the front row, on the counterpane of an undisturbed bed, with her head propped up on two pillows, lies a strange figure, fully dressed, but with her feet hidden under a pad of wadding. An old lady, sitting near this young girl, or rather child, tells me her harrowing story.

This little girl has gangrene in both feet. They decided to send her to Lourdes, but no one would stay in the carriage with her, so fetid was the odour of her ulcers; pus was so abundant as to break through all her linen dressings, and a bucket had to be placed under her; her sufferings were so acute that her cries drowned the train whistles; and at one time this good lady, not knowing how to relieve her, and having agreed to remain in that compartment alone with her, undid her dressings and put her feet out of the window to cool them in the fresh air.

The poor child was taken out at Lourdes without being able to have them wrapped up again, for the least touch made her scream; she took her first bath in the piscina this morning, and one minute afterwards the sores dried up and became painless; she now endures, and without feeling it, this layer of wadding, and the lady lifts it up and says: "Look, sir." And on her feet, which were no longer, or not yet, feet, I saw two dull red sponges, but dry sponges. There was neither matter nor blood nor smell—there was nothing of any kind. "After a few more baths our Lady will cure her altogether," says the lady with a smile.

I look at the child and vainly seek to discover what she is thinking; her expression is taciturn and appears to suggest an inward shrinking; the eyes are speaking, but what are they saying? They tell of infinite resignation, of a sort of indifference about herself: they are both far away and grieving, and, above all, very grave. Is she lost in God, or only stupefied by the sudden change from intolerable suffering to a most sweet repose? I cannot tell.

On the other hand, what a delightful person is this little old woman, how refined and distinguished, and how devoted to her sick charge! At her advanced age, she has undergone the fatigue of a long journey to help this poor cripple for life, not of her own station, whom she hardly knows at all, and she tells you about it all so simply, she thinks what she has done so natural, that you are really touched to hear her; she asks me to come and see her protégée again and to pray for her. Yes, indeed; anything you will, dear good Samaritan!

Good Abbé Darros, one of the chaplains who acts as chaplain at the hospital, fetches me to assist at the meals of the sick. Here I am back in the corridors, in which ladies are running to and fro, some to empty basins, others to bring back bowls of soup; and here they are summoning stretcher-bearers to help up an impotent man who is too heavy; and there one of them pulls up the chaplain to tell him that the bedridden patient she is in charge of is about to die and it is time to give him extreme unction; so we go to see her patient, and the chaplain, accustomed as he is to the appearances assumed by the dying, reassures the lady, whose sad face relaxes; and there is a continual coming and going amidst the conversations of those who stop the way everywhere with their talks. However, at last we get free from the crowd and come to the great refectory.

It is so full that the guests are packed together at table like a barrel of fish, elbow wedged into elbow. Young girls and ladies in fresh, clean dresses beneath their aprons are helping everyone with a plate of soup, a slice of mutton and haricot-beans, and are pouring out wine from stoneware jugs into their glasses, adding a dash of water to it. There are all sorts of people in this dining-hall adorned with nothing but a crucifix; there are sick folks who look quite well and lunch with an appetite, and others just nibble, their deeply lined faces betraying the persistence of disease; there are others, again, with their heads swathed deftly in linen bandages, doubtless concealing swellings or sores; and others, heaving up and down goitres which keep time to the working of their jaws while they eat; and yet the affections seen here are only such as are presentable.

And the same things are to be met with in the shed outside. There the Belgian colony has installed itself, and all round the tables blonde young women in white caps are talking and laughing and enlivening the afflicted as they wait on them; a little farther on, beneath stretched tarpaulins, there is an encampment of ambulances of sick cases, whom ladies are helping to spoonfuls and morsels of food; and, lastly, in the courtyard, in a sort of waste-ground, is the side table of the monstrosities.

The leonine and mealy jaws, which one might have hoped would have disappeared with the wear and tear of past ages, are to be once more discovered there. Here are lepers sitting cheek-by-jowl alongside of tumorous necks from the uplands; and here are women suffering from lupus, who, if they raise their black veils, exhibit death's heads with two red holes for eyes and a bleeding trefoil instead of a nose; others, who are eaten up with cancer of the face, have only half of their faces left; and, that any liquid he takes may not run away, escaping through the screen of his perforated palate, one poor creature is obliged to fling his head backwards and pinch his nose in order to drink.

In another corner a man suffering from adenitis swells out to the girth of a pumpkin from his ear down to his neck. Under the weight his head bends over, and he swallows his quantum leaning down on one side.

But in this *Cour des Miracles*[1] there are worse things still. A peasant belonging to the pilgrimage from Coutances is taking his lunch by himself, with his face to the wall, like a punished child; and now he turns round to ask for bread . . . Oh!

From a shapeless and slimy hole, which was once a mouth, hangs an enormous tongue. The slack and violet-coloured skin which covers it, like a coating of gum, is apparently dead, but it moves and is alive inside. The man's cheeks and the hair on them drop down, but his chin is—where? How can he swallow? And yet he masticates his meat, but in secret, for his tongue, full of an indescribable something that shakes about, is dropping with lupus!

Dear Lord, remember, in spite of this, that thou, in order to redeem us, didst clothe thyself with the livery of our flesh, and if it be only for the sake of man's wretched body that thou hast sanctified by taking it upon thyself, have mercy on this man and heal him!

Think of the likeness of the Holy Face; it was sorrowful and bloodstained, but it was not repulsive! Save

---

1 A Paris rendezvous where beggars met and shed their simulated diseases. It was suppressed in the reign of Louis XIII.

the very dignity of thy likeness by a miracle, and cleanse and purify this face of its defilement!

"He is appalling," says the chaplain; and then he tells how perplexed he was this morning, when he had to give the poor fellow Holy Communion, for he did not know in which opening of the cavern to put the Host!

"It is believed to be a special sort of cancer," he says. "But come"; and then he takes me to the ambulance yard and stops in front of quite a small child. From the bottom of the leather hood emerges the charming face of a little girl, a blonde of delicate features, and with so fine a skin that the blue network of her veins shows beneath it. A young lady, sitting on a folding stool, is at her side and laughing with her; this child is not suffering, at any rate.

"What is the matter with her? Look, sir."

And the young lady shows us something that was never a body at all, for the child had come into the world rickety and twisted together; her legs are two thin vine-stocks, twisting round one another like the branches of a thyrsis; her arms are like matches with fingers of gelatine, so that they can be turned about in all directions like a kid-glove. As for the rest of her body, it' is but a tiny parcel of pale and boneless flesh. How can she live, built as she is in this fashion?

It is nevertheless true that, if she can neither walk nor move, she vegetates sadly in a hospital from which this excellent young lady has fetched her away to bring her to Lourdes; and one is aware of the deep affection she has devoted to the poor orphan, who, for her part, never takes her eyes off her, becoming as restless as a little lost bird as soon as her friend goes away from her.

It must be admitted that this hospital is both a hell for the body and a paradise for the soul. Nowhere have I seen, alongside the most frightful evils, so much charity and goodwill. From the point of view of human pity, Lourdes is a miracle; there, more than anywhere else, you find the Gospel being put into practice, and a kind of devout woman very unlike those who grow sour in our churches for the purpose of arranging their sorry affairs with the statues of Saints and the money boxes attached to them.

I was turning over such thoughts on my way through the iron railings when I met a stretcher-bearer whom I knew. We walk together down the street and pace up and down between the shops where they sell rosaries. A gang of Belgians is passing by, and my friend says:

"The Belgians are the only ones here who are splendidly organised; under the terrace of the Rosary they have set up an Enquiry Office, and first-aid is in perpetual readiness; the reports of their sick, provided with doctors' certificates and very carefully checked, are models of their kind. As administrators they are perfect, but as men—well, that is another matter.

"At Lourdes they are a band apart. As for us, when we are summoned to lend a hand, we go without troubling whether the pilgrim in need of a bearer or a bath is a Frenchman or not. But it is not so with them; they will help none but Belgians; their pity is patriotic and their charity national."

"It looks, however, as if the egoism and the love of ease, which they have brought with them to Lourdes during recent years, have not turned to the benefit of their sick, for although during their first pilgrimages they obtained numerous and notable cures, now they get far fewer. Formerly they travelled here third-class and never left the bedridden; today they have a specially built medical train with first-class compartments and sleeping-cars, and a chapel for the celebration of Mass on the journey; all is the very height of comfort; and then, once landed here and having lodged their helpless cases, half the sick-attendants of both sexes scamper off on excursions into the mountains. In a word, they have turned their pilgrimage into a pleasure-party; and most surely these new ways are not winning approval up there."

"But," I answer, "we must take intentions into account. As practical folks, the Belgians wanted to avoid the painful horror of trainloads of dying people being dragged from one end of France to the other in penitential railway-carriages—the sinister 'white trains' so well described by Zola—and they desired to have their sick better provided for that they might suffer less. Such comfort, then, from that point of view, is an act of charity."

"Perhaps; but, nevertheless, there are the facts: ask the people of Lourdes. There is not one who is not struck with the diminution of favours inflicted on the Belgians since they have given up travelling in poverty and abandoned their posts at the pillows of the bedridden to run off in bands in search of diversion."

V

YOU get more attached to certain sick folk whom you don't know at all, than to others with whom you are equally unacquainted: such is the reflection I make to myself on my way to the hospital this morning. These preferences are due to many causes, most of them unconscious. Certainly, one is more moved to pity those who seem to suffer most or are smitten with the most repellent affectations; the thought of them haunts one, indeed, whereas many other sick cases pass unremarked, with their less astounding symptoms, through the marvellous kaleidoscope of afflictions revolving in the hospital, where one moribund case constantly follows another. One is quite evidently, whether one wishes it or not, more sensibly drawn towards a young and pretty but helpless girl than to an old woman, and also more moved by the tortures of a child than by those of a man. I believe that everyone must be measured by this standard of sensibility. Let us further add that there are sympathies undetermined by the more or less marked charm of features, by the difference of sex, and by the more or less pitiable acuteness of sufferings undergone, and that these are felt by some and not by others. You speak to yonder bedridden folk, but feel not the least desire to question their neighbours, and immediately a kind of bond is linked between you, and the special interest you take in those cases is explained; but the reason of your sympathy in such instances is still far from clear; it springs from some impulse which it would be very difficult to analyse. Lastly, in your preference there is sometimes involved a third party, who has a stronger hold upon your heart than the actual patient, but who makes you feel drawn towards the latter by a sort of ricochet.

Such, I believe, is the case of the little girl with the gangrened feet, whom I am going to see once more. In truth, I am far from indifferent as to the fate of this child who has endured the most fearful martyrdom, but I confess that what makes its claim upon me is the heroic self-sacrifice of the old lady who looks after her, and is so pleased for anyone to come for news about her protégée. The little girl is going on better and better; plainly her feet are not what one could call pretty little pettitoes; indeed, were they ever so? but now they are shaped like feet; they are growing lighter, and their dull red is beginning to change to a rose-tint. Unfortunately, she is going away with the pilgrimage with which she came, and I shall not know until next year, supposing she is brought back to Lourdes, whether she has been thoroughly healed. As for the man with the fluctuant tongue, he has left the hospital in the same state as when he came; and the same is the case with the poor thin lath of a child in her tiny ambulance; she was not untwisted in the piscinas; and the charitable young lady has borne her off, happy, after all, in having been able to procure her this excursion into the open-air and the accompanying diversion.

Among the sick who have replaced those who have left the wards on the ground-floor to return by train there are two frightful cases in the women's room. One is that of a wretched woman lying at full length in a frame, and you can see just a fraction of her livid face emerging from the hollow of a pillow with its flaps tucked back; she is affected with general and acute tuberculosis of the bones and lungs, the terrible Pott's disease, which has already warped her spine and covered her hips with suppurating fistulas and abscesses; she is drenched in a pool of pus. The other is that of a young nun from a convent at St Brieuc, who is lying in a wicker basket; she is pretty, and appears to be dead; her cheeks are of an extraordinary pallor, her eyes closed, and her lips of the colour of pumice-stone. A priest, who is a stretcher-bearer, is talking to the nun who is in charge of her; he entangles me in the conversation and tells me that Sister Justinian is twenty-six, and that, after having been attacked by pleurisy followed by haemoptysis, she has been rendered incapable of moving for more than a year by coxalgia accompanied with stiffness of the joints and deformation of the lower limb. Her leg is enclosed in a plaster cast, and her state of exhaustion is such that it is amazing that she manages to keep alive.

In the men's ward, which I am traversing, there are cases of cancer of a straw-tinted pallor, consumptives with watery eyes, and an old fellow whose bronzed face reveals Addison's disease, some paralytics, and some who drag themselves along on crutches; there are few with ulcers—at any rate, of a visible kind—but there is a sort of leprosy that puffs out the face of a man whose skin looks like grained leather worked over with a punch.

I go to the first floor. In one of the rooms occupied by the pilgrimage from Belley, which has just arrived and is settling in, the Sisters of the Holy Ghost are hurrying about: they are attired in the splendid habit of the Beaune hospital nuns—belonging to the same order—a blue costume with enormous sleeves and the tight wrist-bands and the white linen hennin,[1] the full dress of the fifteenth-century nuns. One of them is comforting a weeping child, whose leg is confined in a wooden gutter; he is like the little nun down below, tuberculous and coxalgic, with eruptions of abscesses on his legs and reins. The sister tells me that the journey was a painful one, not owing to the child, but because one of the consumptives in the compartment almost died in the train, of a sudden spitting of blood; and she adds that they have now to take their sick home cured; and how she hopes for it, charming old sister that she is, with her clear and open expression and her faint sweet smile.

I leave her, and, in a passage, come across two blind patients, one of whom has his eyes in a sort of soft roe of fried fish and the other is in a stout bung of ichor. They are led by an ophthalmic patient who sees clearly

---

1 The *hennin* is a high conical head-dress worn by French women from 1430-1465.

enough to find his way, but his eyeballs are retorted and exude, from their edges of bleeding ham, trails of tears down his cheeks. As I look at them, I am haunted with the memory of old Breughel's picture, in which the fumbling movements and appearances of various kinds of blindness are so well depicted. Now I enter another room; and there, among the bedridden brought by the Dutch, appears a real gnome, a little boy stuffed beneath a blanket, fully clothed and wearing a Tyrolese hat of green felt.

His head is that of a hunchback; it is as white as if it were lime-washed, and without the least expression of any lines upon it. Lying stretched upon his back, with his protruding chest bulging up beneath the blanket and his thin, slender limbs, he looks like a frog. He appears to be insensible and wrapped in a sort of coma. When I enquire what has brought him to such a state, they simply reply: "His spinal column is decayed."

As for the other invalids belonging to the same pilgrimage and gathered together in the same room, they are incurable cases of scrofula and other infirmities, but such as may continue to live on.

Here there is an odour of nastiness and nausea: I feel that I must have a change of air, and, leaving the hospital, I run right into a pilgrimage singing in dusty and drawling tones:

> "From our home in Vienne,
>   All thy lovers we come:
> O Mary, be Queen
>   In our home, in our home!"

While I am watching the heavy and lagging lout-ishness of these men and women and listening to the childish and indolent tune of their hymn, I have no difficulty in identifying these pilgrims as belonging to the subordinate race of Poitou.

To avoid them I flee by another road, and on my way I say to myself what must be said by everyone after he has seen so much wretchedness and so many ills pass before him at the hospital: Lord, how good art thou not to have inflicted such diseases as these upon me! Certainly, we must go to Lourdes, if we want to realise what the mouldering rags of our poor human bodies may become. There is not a single Clinic that can show such a varied inventory of monstrosities. You run over in memory the fabulous beasts of the Middle Ages, but what are they compared with the bleeding death's-head of the man with lupus and the swollen tongue that protrudes from the peasant of Coutances?

I go to the Record Office.[1] After the disheartening scene at the hospital, shall I there find the joyful sight of the patient who has sprung forth from the piscina miraculously healed? Beneath the arches of the terrace this Office fills a small building lighted by windows with coloured panes, stoutly protected from the crowd by iron bars and surmounted with a marble statue of St Luke.

---

1 *Bureau des Consolations:* A medical registry where the doctors' certificates of sick patients, and the history of their cases and claims to be cured, are examined and tested and put on record with the verdict of the medical examiners.

The inside, which is rather dark, is lined from top to bottom of the walls and on its arched ceiling with panelling of cheap deal, and reminds you of a ship's cabin. Between the two windows on the side of the Esplanade is a large table, and another runs at right angles to it; and nailed to the wall between the windows is a crucifix; opposite is a fireplace, on the mantelpiece of which there is a statue of Our Lady of Lourdes; to the left is a door opening into another small room, which is used for the medical examinations; to the right are photographs of the miraculously healed in a frame, and opposite the entrance door is another, opening behind the terrace upon the broad walk along the Gave; some benches, a few arm-chairs, some ordinary chairs, and some cupboards containing the files and registers—I verily believe that is all.

Before the large table sits Dr. Boissarie, and to his left at another table is his colleague, Dr. Cox. One's first impression, when assisting at the questioning of the sick, is that Dr. Boissarie is an examining magistrate, but a brusque and cheery one, cross-examining the accused with a good-tempered smile; and then the amiable Dr. Cox seems to play the part of a recorder, and, while he is writing, he now and then gives a glance at the culprit, and puts down his answer, if required.

The fact is, with all due deference to those who know nothing of the Lourdes clinic except by hearsay, that these two practitioners are very much on their guard, and that they put on record but very few of the extraordinary cases which pass through their hands.

As soon as I get in, Dr. Boissarie signals to me to take a seat near him, and he goes on calmly talking to a young girl of somewhat strange appearance, a case of paralysis, who declares that she was miraculously cured this morning after her first bath. She does not belong to any pilgrimage, and has no doctor's certificate, nor any evidence of her antecedents; she is extremely reticent on many points, and says nothing as to the origin of her malady; but she has to deal with a man of great patience, who leads her to contradict herself, and says to her: "Come, you must have had some such treatment as this; you had such symptoms as these"—and at last he ends by extracting the truth from her by making her acknowledge that she is subject to fits, and that then she has to have four men to hold her, and the doctor smiles and dismisses her with a few kind words, and says to me: "A bit of counterfeit coin."

And then come others, showing some amelioration but not cured. "Come now, walk a little way without your crutches." And the man tries to take a few steps down the room, stops exhausted, and is given a chair. They ask how long he is going to stay at Lourdes, and invite him to return for a final examination before going away.

And so on. One can truly bear witness that the Record Office does not try to push forward the miraculous, for any affection that may be due to any disorder of the nervous system is set aside at the outset; and as for other cases, no final verdict is given until a few years afterwards, when there has been time to make sure that the cure has been maintained. Unfortunately, such prudent procedure is not that of the press; it takes just the opposite course to that of the clinic, and, so far as miracles which are not miracles are concerned, justifies the criticism that is obliged to take nothing but necessarily incorrect reports as its foundation. If we are to believe the correspondents of Catholic papers who have been sent to attend the pilgrimages, miracles abound in swarms; they vie with one another as to who will see most. If this were really the fact, the uncured would be the exception, and the miraculously healed would be no exception at all.

"Do you know Madame Rouchel?" asks Dr. Boissarie.

"No."

"Well, I will show her to you presently, for she is now at Lourdes, and I am expecting her this morning." And then he reminds me, as he looks through a report, that they are bringing him the declared miracle—a genuine one this time—of a case of lupus cured instantaneously, and the disease has never recurred since 1903, when the cure took place.

I look through the report with him; it is crammed with records and medical certificates. Before coming here, this woman had been examined by all the doctors of Lorraine and treated by all the specialists in skin-diseases; all the certificates were agreed in concluding that it was impossible to cure a case of lupus so far advanced.

What had been tried to arrest the progress of the ulcer was incredible. They had ravaged the unfortunate woman's jaw by pulling out her teeth; they had cauterised her without stint, and the lupus, nevertheless, went on devouring her alive and spreading an odour so nauseating that no one had the courage to dress her wounds. Her face had become something frightful. Nose and mouth coalesced and opened up a red crater whence flowed streams of sulphur-tinted lava; her cheeks were pierced with two holes as wide as a little finger, and they had to be stopped with plugs of wadding when the poor woman was preparing to eat or drink, so that food and liquids might not escape through these openings. Her state had become so dreadful that she had determined to fling herself into the river. Abbé Hamann, a priest of the church of St Maximin at Metz, where she lived, prevented her from doing so, and had her enrolled among the sick of the pilgrimage which the town was sending to Lourdes.

On arriving at the Grotto she prays, and then bathes what she has of her face in the piscina. Next day she again begins soaking her face with a sponge, but with no greater success. That same day, in her shame, feeling that she is a source of disgust to everybody, during the 4 p.m. procession of the Blessed Sacrament on the Esplanade, she is unwilling to take her place in the ranks of the sick and conceals herself in the Rosary, which is now empty, behind the high altar. On her knees she was reading her prayers in a missal, when, after the procession, Mgr. de Saint Dié, who was carrying the monstrance, returns to replace it in the church. Just then the bandage covering her face comes undone and falls on her book, which gets spotted with blood and matter. She ties it on firmly once more with a double knot, and, fearing the return of the crowd in the wake of the bishop, she flies from the church and goes off to the spring to take a little water. She is bending down over the tap when the bandage once more comes undone. Rather astonished—for she was certain she had fastened it securely—she readjusts it and returns to the hospital, where she complains of its failure to hold, and asks to have it put on more carefully. They take it off, and the two who have removed it cry out: "You are cured!" She could not believe it; she had to see her face in a glass to be convinced that the lupus had disappeared at a stroke, in a second. Her face was made good again, her nose was more or less restored, and the open holes in her palate and cheeks were stopped; her flesh had recovered spontaneously.

And just as we were talking of this unheard-of phenomenon, in walks the woman and bows to the doctor with a smile. She may be fifty-four; she is stout and walks heavily; and she looks like a peasant, a woman who lets chairs in a church. I observe her face, which looks as if it were formerly burnt; it is blurred with rosy patches and veined with white; the traces of her scars are plainly apparent. Clearly she is an ugly woman, but her ugliness is not repellent.

And while the doctors who happen to be in the Office are examining her, I talk with Dr. Boissarie of that other case of lupus of which Zola himself saw the cure at Lourdes, the case of Mlle Marie Lemarchand of Caen, who, under the name of Elise Rouquet, is one of the characters in his book. The cure took place on August 20, 1882, and like that of Mme Rouchel, which came after it, it was instantaneous.

But she was conscious of her cure when it occurred. No sooner had she applied lotions to herself at the piscina than she felt terrible pains, and then was at once certain that she was cured; and so, indeed, she was. Dr. d'Hombres, who was there and had noticed her while she was bathing the horrible hash of her face, and had examined her immediately after she had left the piscina, made this declaration quite clearly: "Instead of the hideous sore, I saw a dry surface, apparently covered afresh with new skin."

Zola refused to acknowledge the spontaneous character of the cure which, however, he had himself witnessed; he preferred to say that the appearance of the face improved gradually and that the cure proceeded indolently; he invented stages and degrees so as not to be compelled to confess that this sudden restoration of a ruined face was beyond the laws of nature; for that would have meant admitting that it was a miracle.

And that is just the point. Though it is quite possible for lupus, which is so refractory to all kinds of medical treatment, nevertheless to disappear after a longer or shorter interval; yet neither the old method nor the more recent therapeutics of luminous rays have driven or will drive it away, or make it vanish in the twinkling of an eye, as if by enchantment. In such a case, the miraculous element lies less in the cure itself than in its rapidity and instantaneity.

The story of Marie Lemarchand, as told by Zola, is therefore deliberately inaccurate. Anxious to provide the opponents of the supernatural with arguments, he slipped into his book not only the fabricated retardation of the cure, but suggested that the lupus might have been a false lupus of nervous origin. What follows? Suppose this is admitted, how is the matter in question altered? The principal point would remain— that of the sudden restoration of the cells and tissues. I presume that an unsettlement of the nerves could not suddenly make the flesh grow again; what then? The fact is quite the contrary: Marie Lemarchand's lupus had a perfectly well-known origin; it was certified by the doctors and proved by the very state of the patient, for she was affected with consumption when she came to Lourdes. The cause of her lupus, like that of the majority of such cases, was tuberculous. We may add that the tubercles of her lungs vanished at the same time as her facial ulcers. The Virgin had killed two birds with one stone. Twelve years have passed away, and neither of her maladies has recurred. Hence, it may be affirmed that Mlle Marie Lemarchand has been miraculously and truly healed.

I now think of the similar and yet differing cases of these two women. Mme Rouchel experienced no disturbance and felt none of the hot or cold spasms which are so often the precursory signs of cures at Lourdes; she was healed without suffering and without knowing it, apart from the prayers of the crowd and the piscinas, alone, and in a corner. Mlle Lemarchand, on the other hand, suffered frightfully in the piscina, and was fully conscious that she was healed; and she did not retain, as did Mme Rouchel, any traces of scars or wounds; she had no white seams nor reddish patches, and her face became just as it was before.

I am driven from such reflections by the noise of the talk of those who meet in crossing one another in the room, which has gradually filled up. Doctors and priests and sight-seers crowd in; the secretary of the Bishop of Tarbes, courteous Father Eckert, enters and begs for information for the *Journal de la Grotte* of which he is the editor, and he takes his place close to Dr. Cox. Again the door opens, and a young girl, accompanied by two ladies, asks to have her case examined.

What is her name? Virginie Durand, aged 19, living at Saint-Michel Chef-Chef in Loire-Inférieure. She says that she was consumptive and was cured last year. Dr. Cox rises and goes to fetch the papers and records; he finds her name, and reads the evidence aloud.

From this it is ascertained that Virginie Durand came with the pilgrimage from Nantes last year; she presented a medical certificate testifying that she was suffering from tuberculosis of the lungs; her spittle had been analysed, and there was no doubt as to the nature of her malady. She had often been subject to haemoptysis, and had become so weak that she could not stand. When plunged into the bath, she had suffered alarming pains, and almost expired in an attack of sudden suffocation; and then, before she was taken out of the water, she felt her tortures give way to an ineffable sense of well-being; and she was able to dress without assistance and go to the Grotto unaided, to eat with a good appetite, and to sleep. She was sounded the very same day, and no trace of any lesion was detected.

"Has your doctor provided you with any fresh certificate?" asks Dr. Boissarie. She hands him one, and states that she has never been ill since she returned to her own country, and that she has gained twenty-seven pounds in weight.

"Will you examine the young lady?" suggests the doctor to several medical men who are walking round the late invalid. Two undertake the work, and sound her in the adjoining room, and on returning they declare that her lungs reveal no abnormal symptoms.

Dr. Cox adds the new certificate to the record, makes a note of the consultation, and when the young girl comes once more to Lourdes next year, she will be examined to ascertain whether her cure is still maintained.

There are some who have thus come for fifteen years in succession, by way of thanksgiving, to the Grotto, and they presented themselves at the clinic so that their state of health can be followed year by year. Real family archives, indeed, are these archives of Lourdes!

"Well, gentlemen," suddenly exclaims Dr. Boissarie, "here is an interesting case which we closely studied a few days ago. Come in, my child; come in, and sit down there."

And standing up amidst the suddenly silent room, he says as he points to a young girl sitting in an armchair:

"Mlle Rosalie Monnier who is now here belongs to the pilgrimage of the diocese of Belley, and she comes from the village of Cuet. There was born the Blessed Pierre Chanel, a Marist Father who, as you know, was martyred in 1840 in Oceania. His memory has given rise to a fervent cultus in that village; and you will see that these particulars are not altogether irrelevant.

"Mlle Monnier belongs to a family of agriculturists, who had six children, of whom two have died of consumption. She, at the age of sixteen, fell into a languishing sickness arising from some indefinite cause, and this stopped her growth, and has been complicated for about nineteen years past with such a dyspeptic condition that she has been obliged to take nothing but milk in quantities insufficient to nourish her; furthermore, to keep from vomiting, she has been forced to make use of an India rubber tube to swallow it.

"The doctors, whose certificates we have here, have given up all treatment of the case; she has been confined to her room and unable to endure either light or noise, and for some time she was so weak from inanition that once they thought she would die and administered Extreme Unction.

"But she shared the devotion of her district, its devotion to the Blessed Pierre Chanel. Being given up by medical science, which declared itself capable of effecting even alleviation, she entrusted her case to him, and after ardently invoking him, she felt suddenly and intuitively that she would be cured by the Virgin, if she went to Lourdes. She started on September 6, and the long twenty-six hours' journey was as fatiguing as it possibly could be; she suffered from sickness as far as Lyons, arrived at Lourdes fasting on the evening of the next day, and there was put in the hospital of Notre-Dame des Sept Douleurs. On the 8th, early in the morning, she dragged herself to the hospital chapel, invoked the Blessed Pierre; and was borne to the Grotto where she received Holy Communion. At once she felt as if she were being inwardly torn asunder—that, to use her own words, she was being opened like a book—and from that moment she has not suffered any more, and eats whatever is given to her with a good appetite. She is still rather pale, but her recovery has been going on for some days, and that visibly.

"I have considered it my duty to let the clergy present know—because it may be of interest for the canonization of the Blessed Pierre Chanel which is now being submitted to the Congregation of Rites at Rome—that the intervention of that martyr with the Virgin is claimed for this cure.

"I may further add that we have been able twice already to testify to his role as a mediator with the Immaculate Conception at Lourdes; once, with regard to one of his compatriots, Vion-Duty, an incurably blind man, who after a novena bathed his eyes with the water of the spring and immediately recovered his sight; and, the other time, with regard to a woman of the pilgrimage from Belley who invoked him in the chapel of the hospital of Notre-Dame, and was cured the same day after communicating at the Grotto.

"So far as concerns the affliction of Mlle Monnier, I call the attention of my confreres to the conditions in which her cure took place. Could this young girl have been cured solely by natural means after her nineteen years of illness? Plainly, yes. Theoretically it may be maintained that she could, but not in one minute and during the time of a single communion; for, just as nature cannot cicatrise an open wound in a second, so can it not suddenly renew a constitution undermined by nineteen years of inanition. Such instantaneity of effect must especially strike you, for, as you know, it is not in our power to do without convalescence and to pass directly from a state of grave illness to health without any transition.

"For my own part, I think that this cure—if it should prove enduring—has taken place without a bath or a glass of water, apart from the crowd and without any outcries or the blessing of the Blessed Sacrament, which demonstrates how false are all the hypotheses that attribute the cures of Lourdes to shock produced by the cold water and suggestion arising from the clamour of the mobs. In any case, how various are the ways in which people get cured, if they are to be cured, at Lourdes!"

VI

THE ugliness of everything one sees here ends by being unnatural, for it falls below the known low-water marks. Man, of himself, and apart from any suggestion emanating from the dismal regions of the damned, could never have been induced to dishonour God in this fashion. At Lourdes there is such a plethora, such a flux of base and bad taste that one cannot get away from the idea of an intervention of the Most Base.

Leaving aside the Basilica which seems to shiver, lean as a pole, under its clown's cap, in its spare stone vesture, on the damp flatness of its rock, what can be said of the Rosary, the dropsical circus which swells out and bulges up beneath its feet? How can we define the latter building, the interior of which vaguely reminds us of the ace of clubs, with five altars arranged within the circumference of each of its leaves? We should like to hear to what style it belongs, for it contains something of everything, of the Byzantine and the Romanesque, of the Hippodrome and the Casino; but if we look closer, there is above all else something of the machinery store and of the rotunda for locomotives; only the rails and the central turn-table are wanting, instead of the high altar, to enable the engines to come out of the side-wings and to perform their evolutions on the broad walks of the Esplanade, whistling to the disc.[1]

And this rotunda, which should be smoky with the fumes of steam-coal and pitch-black with layers of soot, is as white as fresh plaster; they began decorating it like the hall of a theatre, though the scene-painting is unfinished; but everywhere there are ornaments of imitation gold, electric candelabra, heavy and twisted, with the insolence of an atrocious luxury; columns, which are nothing but square and stunted hunks of wall, furnished with marble plaques half-way up, about the colour of minced pork, on which the ex-votos, inscribed with sunk golden letters, are happily scarcely visible; by way of capitals, above these squat pillars, run verses of litanies cut out in the foliage, and they rise, bending in curves, to reach a dome distempered with chalky milk, pierced with bull's-eyes adorned with God knows what kind of glass! Then small columns taper upwards, and at the top of their stems flowers a bunch of feather blooms, or rather there are diadems of plumes of savage chiefs; that, indeed, belongs to the barbaric gaudiness of opera, to the Alhambra of the provinces. In the incoherence of the whole, next imagine such quack-show decorations as those afforded by hundreds of electric bulbs lit up at night, with their shattering gleams refracted from the gilding and the

---

1 *Disque*, a flat metal disc painted a different colour on each side, used on French railways to signal whether the line is clear or blocked.

marbles of the walls, and you may believe yourself to be anywhere you like except in a church.

This nave or crypt—one shrinks from finding a name for these queer-shaped halls—is clearly the product of the imagination of a gambler in luck and a beadle in delirium; but there is worse to come. The builder of this religious casino was a man of genius compared with the artists.

They believed it was their duty, indeed, to order for the altar-niches immense pictures executed—for the sake of obtaining what was most sumptuous and expensive—in mosaics carried out by Italian manufacturers of coloured cements.

And in this they have surpassed one's wildest dreams. Art, even at its lowest, has nothing to do with what is here. It is not even bad art, for in art itself can be found the bad; you can explain and define it; its very discussion implies the recognition perhaps of some endeavour, or, at any rate, of some infirmity or mistake; but these walls of pebbles, cemented closely together in a ground crammed with gold crevices and reproducing hazy frescoes bearing the signatures of poor unconscious designers, can but suggest the thought of matchless unskilfulness and inanity; it is not even queer, it is not even mad; it is puerile and doddering; it is mere discord and dotage. In the presence of this Nativity, this Annunciation, this Garden of Olives, and this Flagellation, your hands drop down; the lowest pupil in the School of Fine Art would have done better. Indeed, here there is no question of talent, but of the A B C and the rudiments; here there is ignorance of one's craft aggravated with the silly sentimentalism of some working-man member of a Catholic club who has had a drop too much!

And so one takes refuge before the only panel that has been entrusted, in a moment of distraction, no doubt, to a painter of mediocre quality, I grant, but yet to a painter. This man, at least, knew how to draw and paint. Anyone may dispute M. Maxence's advertising and chromographic style of art, and think that his "Ascension," reduced to scale, would be just the thing for a confectioner's comfit-boxes, but his art indeed is true art if it is compared with the infantile decrepitudes of the three others.

And the same reflection occurs to you when looking at a Virgin by Maniglier, whose design fills the tympanum over the door. She is holding a child who is giving St Dominic on his knees a rosary, the beads of which used to be feigned by little electric bulbs lighted up at night! In a Paris exhibition it would be thought cheap and savouring of the soap trade, and not at all religious, but there it flashes forth amazingly amidst the infernal freaks of the Raffl stores.

What bishop affected with ablepsia, what ecclesiasts urged on by the powers of evil, can have ordered and accepted such things?

And they have ordered and have accepted worse still. To say nothing of the painted cast-iron Virgin on the Esplanade, aureoled with a circle of electric almonds, with a head like a ray's and milky eyes and livid cheeks, looking like some demented creature's who has just escaped from a lunatic-asylum; if you want to know to what a point acute ugliness may attain, climb up the zigzags on the slope of the Espelugues, where they have begun to set up a Way of the Cross. One Station has been erected on a knoll surrounded with trees.

Here invective breaks down. Fancy some statues taken from a Way of the Cross such as they sell in the Rue Bonaparte or the Rue Saint-Sulpice, magnified to twice the size of nature, and set down in the open-air and outlined against the sky in full daylight.

In their midst is seated a good fellow, whose face might be the seat of a pair of breeches if it were not for the two eyes, and around this enormously overgrown doll some supernumeraries with insipid and hard features and petrified gestures are encircling a statue standing up in a white garment, thrusting forward the regular outlines of the masculine head in a hair-dyer's advertisement, with the beard white on one side and black on the other. And this is meant for our Lord standing before Pilate! And then imagine, to give a touch of animation to the motionless array of dead puppets, some living and bewildered peasant-women who first of all see nothing but Pilate seated in a prominent position, apart from the bands around, and honestly mistake him for Jesus Christ, and go forward to embrace him and make him touch their rosaries. Then you will have some conception of this odious masquerade of the Scriptures!

This is the only Station of the Way of the Cross now erected. A good Curé told me that money was wanting for the erection of the rest, and he seemed to think they would find it hard to obtain enough to order the remainder of these divine desecrations from Raffl. Let him take comfort! I should know nothing of my fellow-Catholics, if I doubted for a second whether they would joyfully allow themselves to be stripped for the delight of completing such a work!

Evidently, in no place, in no country, and at no time, has anyone dared to exhibit such sacrilegious horrors, and if one reflects that they were made expressly for Lourdes, manufactured expressly for our Lady, one comes to draw, from such a spectacle as this, this lesson.

There is no doubt that such wicked attempts must be attributed to the vindictive pranks of the devil. It is his vengeance upon Her whom he abhors, and one may well hear him say:

"I am on your track, and wherever you stay I will take my stand. You shall never be rid of my presence. At Lourdes you may get all the prayers you please, you may think you have returned to the fair days of the Middle Ages: crowds will flock to you; the cheers for the miracles, the Magnificats for the cures, the cease-less rumble of the rosaries may do you homage as they will do nowhere else; that may be. In an age which I am working upon and perverting in my own way, you may perhaps discover some sanctity among the souls that lie scattered at your feet; that, too, may happen. But art, which is the only fine thing in the world after sanctity, you shall not only have to go without, but I shall so arrange as to have you insulted without res-pite by the perpetual blasphemy of Ugliness. I will so darken the understanding of your bishops and priests and people that it will never occur to them to take away the permanent chalice of my insults from your lips! All that represents you and your Son shall be grotesque; all that depicts your angels and your saints shall be base. You will ascertain, too, that I have left nothing out; I have even borne in mind the things connected with worship, especially those that touch the very Flesh of Christ most nearly. I have paid special attention to the monstrances and ciboria, and have determined that they shall be sumptuous atrocities. But the singular abomination of the religious jewellery of Europe has not satisfied me; you were perhaps accustomed to it, but I have found something better; I have requisitioned the *rastas*[1] of South America, and they have understood me. I am really pleased with the frightful things they offer you. Just look at the works in your treasury at Lourdes, for I myself have chosen them, one by one!"

And these words afford evidence of a disconcerting truth, when one considers the aesthetics of Lourdes! Art, indeed, is a special gift which man uses as he will, well or ill, but which nevertheless retains, however profane it may be, the divine character of being a gift. Among the various appearances that touch the soul and affect the senses, it is the reproduction of the Beautiful in its uniqueness and multiformity, which it, to some extent, represents in its faint mirror, for infinite Beauty,

---

1 *Rasta* is a popular abbreviation from *rastaquouère* (= *leather-dragger*), the nickname of a Venezuelan general who had bullock-hides tied behind the horses of his mounted men, so that the noise might deceive the enemy as to the strength of his troops; the word is also applied to any foreigner living in a showy style, without anyone knowing how he can manage to do it.

inaccessible as it is to fallen natures, is one with God himself.

And Lamennais makes use of very similar expressions for the definition of art when he concludes thus: "Beauty, so far as man can reproduce it in his works, is necessarily related to God."

But if that is the case, the contrary is equally true, and Ugliness, too, is necessarily related to the devil; it reflects him just as Beauty reflects God.

Hence it is plain that when one attributes to Satan what belongs to Christ, when one depicts Jesus and the Virgin in squalid images; in any case, one is playing into his hands; one is practising a sort of black magic by paying homage to the Accursed, when, by reversing the roles and transforming into effigies of the infernal the effigies of the divine, one puts, to his delight, into the Stations of the Cross the ridiculous figures commonly made use of.

Ugliness, ineptitude, the inartistic, as soon as they are applied to Jesus, inevitably become, so far as he who perpetrates them is concerned, sheer sacrilege.

Most Catholics, happily for themselves, know not what they do, for the Evil One makes use of premotion and does not reveal his designs to those whom he incites. He confines himself to utilising the meanness of man's nature and his lack of faith; he acts by means of the country and town clergy, whom he blinds and whose innate vulgarity of taste he increases; to help them, he settles down in the workshops in the district of Saint-Sulpice, and there he inspires his vassals to the prostitution of the divine and organises with their assistance the carnival of the heavenly Jerusalem, the burlesque of heaven itself.

Ah! if only one could exorcise these factories of pietistical products, what weird spectres would fly out!

The plainest inference from this state of things is that everyone who manufactures, everyone who sells, and everyone who buys products of this kind is a case of unconscious possession.

Priests should reflect upon this, and also ponder how far Jewish influence now dominates amongst dealers in devotional articles. Whether converted or not, over and above the passion for profits, it looks indeed as if these tradesmen feel an involuntary impulse to betray the Messiahs over again by selling him under appearances suggested by the devil.

The argument appealed to by certain exceptionally tolerant Catholics, by way of excusing the extreme ugliness that prevails at Lourdes, is truly weak. They claim that it is indispensable for pleasing the people and for drawing the crowd. To begin with, it has never been proved that the people love the ugly rather than the beautiful; it does not know which is which, and that is all; it would be as enthusiastic over a work of beauty, if it were shown one, as over an ugly piece of work; but by way of artistic food and drink they are supplied, under the cloak of religion, with nothing but bully beef and swipes from the canteen!

And besides, was it not for them that the cathedrals were built in the Middle Ages? And were not the statues, the tapestries, the retables, and all the splendid works that now adorn our museums, created to raise the prestige of the Church in their eyes and to help them to pray?

The people admired them genuinely, and very well understood that this splendour was in itself a worship and a supplication offered to God. No doubt their level has fallen since then; they do not know all this now. But whose fault is it, if it be not that of the clergy, whose mission it was to teach them, and who, by an ignorant disdain of all aesthetics, have brought them down to their original state of indifference?

Lourdes, then, is the paragon of a kind of churchy baseness in art, and in its way it is unique; and so that nothing may be wanting in the criminal game there carried on by the Evil One, on the eves of great feasts they illuminate the façade and belfry of the Basilica with tricoloured electric bulbs, and outline in curves of fire the bulging roof of the Rosary, which then becomes a great gingerbread cake sprinkled with red seeds.

To amuse the riff-raff there was only one thing left, and that was to let off fireworks on the hill of the Way of the Cross, and this last folly only just escaped being committed. A wearer of the soutane, from I know not what province, had laid good hold on the idea, and they had to do all they could to stop him from firing something off.

None the less true is it that, even without rockets and bombs, the liturgical feasts of Lourdes resemble the civic celebrations of the fourteenth of July; have I not heard the blare of brass bands and *Ave Marias* played on cornets and trombones? That evening was, indeed, one of suffering for me.

This country, in which triumphs the odious spectacle of such a bravado of divine beauty, has, since the Virgin took up her abode there, furthermore become traversed in all directions by the devil's own main guards.

To tell the truth, the Grotto of Massabielle was his own possession, for it was a desert and ill-omened place into which no one ventured. Its only tenants were two kinds of creatures both belonging to the infernal bestiary of the Middle Ages: the serpents that lodged in its clefts, and the swine which took shelter there, when Paul Larisse, the village swine-herd, pastured them on the banks of the Gave.

Mary swept away this living filth by appearing, but to foul the Grotto afresh, Satan, during the very time of her apparitions, had it defiled at night by frisking pairs; "they played the fool in the Grotto," the peasants used to say, and they knew the scandals connected with it. Then he attacked Bernadette herself while she was in ecstasy, for she heard wild howls and furious cries coming from the Gave behind her and telling her to run away; and, lastly, he tried to disparage the child's revelations by summoning up more or less queer visions in a band of the possessed, with whose aberrations he endeavoured to upset the confidence of the inhabitants.

But soon good sense returned, and Bernadette was listened to. Then he changed his tactics and stirred up a passion for gain in the quarrymen who had turned into hotel-keepers and sellers of rosaries and tapers; they did their level best to plunder the pilgrims.

And after the love of lucre, came temptations of the flesh. Soon the conduct of these mountaineers, which had been honourable when they were poor, became profligate; appointments were made with strangers; liaisons, which were impossible in a small town where everyone must keep watch over himself, were able to flourish freely in the promiscuity of the immense crowds in which you pass unnoticed; in the hurly-burly of the great pilgrimages it was easy to arrange meetings, and rendezvous had nothing to check them. Satan had cause for rejoicing—but, in fine, he secured nothing but ordinary sins and the failings inherent in human nature; he only effected momentary lapses, and such passing offences as are wiped out in penance.

He wanted something more; he planned deeper and more tenacious crimes; and then he manoeuvred under a cloak of piety, and inaugurated a permanent type of blasphemy by implanting the sacrilege of ugliness at Lourdes.

And it is by this atrocious means—which must, however, generally become known after all—that the old Serpent sets at defiance Her who crushes his head, and even wounds her heel!

VII

DURING the last few days the town has become uninhabitable. Previous records of the national pilgrimages have been surpassed. More than forty-five thousand pilgrims are camping out in a town of nine thousand inhabitants; and although the trains have pumped Brittany, Berri, Burgundy, Forez, and Rouergue dry, yet others have flowed back into the basin overfilled with thousands of travellers from every point of the compass and every part of the world, and numerous caravans from abroad are announced.

Where do they lodge? There is not a single hole left in which people are not sleeping on straw mattresses, packed together like sardines; there is not a loft nor a shed into which they are not heaped together. The inhabitants have let even store-rooms and cellars; even the very shanties in the country round have been requisitioned, and those who have left the trains are wandering about, valise in hand, looking for a shake-down. We shall have to arrange for special trains to transport into the neighbouring stations, for a night's rest, the pilgrims whom they will take back on the dawn of the next morning to Lourdes. Needless to say, the shelters of the Rosary terrace are full. When I got there this morning I found, on entering into the immense rooms, such a painful and acrid whiff of hot air that I was beaten back. Everywhere on the ground are mattresses, women sleeping in their clothes, with a pocket-handkerchief over their faces; others are putting on their shoes again; others are yawning with eyes puffed out and sit up and stretch themselves: children are running about and chasing one another; a little girl is weeping; and outside men are having a wash with a little water dipped up in the hollow of their hand and are shaking themselves. One might fancy oneself in a camp of mountebanks—in a gypsy camp. And it is the same thing with the Rosary which they are trying to ventilate by leaving the doors wide open; hundreds have passed the night there on the benches, kept awake by the flashes of the electric light beating upon them, and by the chants until midnight; and then they succumbed at last to fatigue, when all was silent and the Masses began. The sacristans are run off their legs. They have already provided wine and Hosts and altar-linen for over a thousand Masses which have been said tonight in the Rosary, and which will now go on until two in the daytime. They are being celebrated everywhere on altars improvised out of boards, and they extend right up into the great organ-loft; and the priests help one another, and after the communion the server cleans the chalice in place of the celebrant, so that the sacrifice may be over sooner and that he may be served himself in turn, and that without delay. And thus it is in the Basilica, in the Crypt, and in the village church and in the convents, everywhere, indeed, where the semblance of an altar can be erected. It is a regular whirl of Masses at express speed which does not fail to make me rather uneasy; as for the communions of the faithful, they run to an extravagant number—125,000 in this month alone.

Of course, it is plainly impossible to get near the Grotto and the spring; and if one wants to pray and be recollected, the best plan is to stay at home.

Already the pilgrims lodged in the town are filling the Esplanade; they are making queues, like those outside the doors of theatres, before the helpful refuges, around which there is an indescribable welter of disgusting filth; some are returning from the town with bread and sausages and wine; and families, seated on the grass, are taking a snack together; it is like a Sunday in the Bois de Vincennes, with the sherds of broken bottles and greasy scraps of paper all around.

And now, in a dusty hurly-burly, advances an army of women, emitting hoarse cries and gesticulating. Looking at them more closely, I realise that the four trains expected from Spain have arrived.

Ah! here are the Maugrabins waving their handkerchiefs and kissing their hands to the people, roaring like hyenas!

They are the Children of Mary from Guipuzcoa. I hardly know how to describe these Children of Mary; most of them are short brunettes with large noses and black eyes, with heavy hips and bouncing bustles; and almost all fly a mantilla and play a fan. Some of them are rigged up in costumes that are a compromise between the habit of a nun and the smart dress of a lady in town; two or three wear the raisin-coloured robes of the Carmelites, with a leather belt and an enamelled plate on the body, and these are the Tertiaries of St Teresa; others are dressed in blue and others in black, and these are the Children of the Immaculate Conception and the Children of Our Lady of Compassion; others, again, are accoutred in violet, and there are affiliated members of the Confraternity of the Holy Souls; and, lastly, others are clothed in green, the colour of Our Lady of the Pillar. There are no sick, and very few men in comparison with the multitude of women, but there are many priests smoking cigarettes, while those of the female pilgrims who are not fanning themselves are sucking oranges or crunching sticks of chocolate.

The peaceable frequenters of Lourdes scatter in amazement before this forward push of Spanish women who are greeting them with acclamations. Well, there is no need to worry about these ladies; they will make short work of clearing a way for themselves through the crowd till they get to the Grotto!

Now it is time to go up to the Basilica to hear a Mass. It is stuffed full of people, and I am driven to stay close to the door. By the yellow ribbons in their buttonholes, I recognise these seated on the benches as belonging to the pilgrimage from Holland.

The High Mass begins, and I am astonished to hear it sung in plainchant; it is the only Mass I have ever heard properly sung at Lourdes. After the *Credo* comes a sermon. While the Dutch priest is delivering in the pulpit a discourse which I cannot understand, I once more look round the interior of the Basilica.

It has a scrimped look with its hard groins, thin vaulting and cider-coloured walls; it falls far below the Jesuits' chapel of the Rue de Sèvres, the arrangement of which it somewhat recalls by its crowding together of little side-chapels and cellar-doors opening in the bits of wall that partition them off. Without either elevation or breadth, the nave is almost entirely bordered with a narrow passage in which the crowd jostles but cannot circulate. The deadly duffer who built this wretched pastiche of the thirteenth century succeeded in achieving one thing only—a combination of discomfort and ugliness.

At the end of the nave which culminates in a meagre chevet, which is also surrounded with tiny chapels, there rises, encircled with a gilded grille, an altar of Carrara marble, surmounted with a statue of the Immaculate Conception by Cabuchet, and it is not perceptibly superior to those turned out for the Grotto by Fabisch of Lyons.

No doubt the good Bernadette knew but very little of art, yet she could not help smiling with pity when this same Fabisch showed her his sketches and models. Nevertheless, he went on moulding and hardening his lumps of margarine and boluses of cerate;[1] and when the statue was finished Bernadette, who was consulted to know if it was like the Virgin, answered; "Not at all." Then, some time afterwards, when she saw it set up in the Grotto, she could not help running off at once, since, as we are told by Dr. Douzous, an eyewitness, she could not endure the sight of such an image as that!

---

1 An ointment made of wax and other ingredients.

Let us add, by way of testimony to this most devout man's absolute lack of talent, that he had seen Bernadette in a state of ecstasy, and therefore had seen a human face illumined with a reflection of the divine, and all it resulted in was this effigy of a young first communicant, this vapid and slack personification of insipidity! How little is talent allied to piety in our days! Is it not demonstrated clearly enough in every branch of art?

To return to the Basilica, truly inconceivable is the heap of trashy bric-a-brac and variegated tatters used to adorn it. Everywhere from the walls hang dusty banners, the gold of which has turned to black; and all along the nave, above its pointed arches and beneath its thin windows, the glass of which is coloured like English sugar-plums, decorated with a frieze outlined with metallic hearts making letters of the alphabet and representing the words uttered by the Virgin in speaking to Bernadette, is a profuse display of the flags of all nations: Haiti, Chile, Belgium, England, Austria, Holland, Bolivia . . . and against the walls, everywhere, in the chapels, from top to bottom, there is a collection of ridiculous ex-votos, artificial flowers, wreaths of the newly-married, first communion badges, epaulettes, swords, crosses of the Legion of Honour, pictures of family groups, carpet-work for slippers, and chromos. Only one of these ex-votos is interesting. It is hung up on the right of the choir near the altar dedicated to Notre-Dame de la Salette: it contains, beneath a bulging piece of glass and framed, some fragments of bone and some horrible claws, something like the petrified claws of a leopard. These are the nails of a woman whose arm was paralysed and her hand closed tight for years; her nails had pierced her palm and grown, bent backwards, into the flesh. She plunged her arm into the piscina; it came to life again, and the hand opened and the nails and the decayed bones fell into the bath whence they were fished out.

On inspecting this display of rags fluttering from the ceiling, you would think it was a drying-ground, and that this jumble of trinkets nailed to the walls belonged to a store of reach-me-downs or a bric-a-brac shop; you would certainly suppose they had taxed their ingenuity to house in a Basilica a heap of things which had nothing whatever to do with it. Everything in it is incoherent and incongruous, from the lamp stands in the choir to the candelabra festooned with crystals or Venice glass hanging down the nave. They would be in their proper place in a salon, but not in a church.

It is like a salon overhead, but a stable down below, for in the sanctuary asphalt has been substituted for liturgical paving and tiles.

All this is very ugly. Would that it had been merely simple and naïve, but unhappily that is just what it is not!

Meanwhile, I am grateful to the Dutch for giving me a Mass in pure plainchant, and now I go down to the Rosary, for I have read a notice put up in a corner by one of the doors that the Spaniards, too, are about to celebrate a High Mass, and I am not sorry to be able to see how they carry out their Offices in Spain.

The rotunda of the Rosary, like the Basilica which I have just left, is full. However, I succeed in getting through the hedge of backs and reach a corner. Thence I dive into the field of mantillas which stretches to the steps of the communion-rails; all the Spanish women are crouching down and fanning themselves; the Mass begins with deacon and subdeacon, and the small men's choir, which the priests have brought with them, strikes up the *Introit*.

Good open-hearted Spaniards, they, too, are singing plainchant! The *Introit* is followed by a *Kyrie* unknown to our office-books, but with a strange and supplicatory movement; the *Gloria* and the *Gradual* are of a perceptibly less ancient type; and as for the *Credo*, after beginning in the Gregorian mode, it ends at a bound in Palestrina style; this is clearly by way of transition to the rest of the Office, which is composed exclusively of seguedillas and trills. In fine, the Mass is a hybrid one, consisting of two parts, but the first is beautiful, at any rate!

After the *Credo* the Bishop of Tarbes, who has just arrived, mounts one of the two pulpits which flank the altar on either side. The altar is sumptuous, but, strange to say, its taste is in a fashion pretty correct, and he greets the pilgrims with a few words of welcome. He speaks with simple and calm directness, pronouncing every word distinctly, and is attentively listened to by a Spanish priest perched up in the pulpit opposite.

When the bishop has finished his discourse, the priest translates it to the congregation. Does he really translate it? I cannot tell. First of all I ask myself in astonishment whatever can be the matter with the fellow; for he completely upsets the olive coloured mask which his razor has outlined in blue on his cheeks, bangs the edges of the pulpit with his fists, throws his arms up to the sky, and bellows like one possessed. What a strange transmutation of a placid talk and a few amiable compliments into a tumultuous harangue, a bit of dramatic clap-trap!

At last he stops, streaming with perspiration, utters a few remarks in a rational tone, and all the Maugrabin women stand up and shout three harsh and strident cheers. Thus do these women compensate themselves for the forced silence they have had to endure while seated, and from the moment of the last Gospel, their exuberance overflows in uniting their voices with those of the choir, in singing the march of St Ignatius—a masculine and rhythmical march, which, given forth in these rugged and acutely high-pitched tones, resounds with a barbarian pomp in violent contrast with the dreadful vulgarity of the hymns usually bellowed here.

One stifles in the rotunda, which is so badly built that it cannot be properly ventilated, and I escape before the rush of the mantillas has had time to bar the doors. Once outside, I find a seat on the benches along the bank of the Gave, and think over the very unliturgical life one has to live at Lourdes.

In the ordinary way, you never hear a plainchant High Mass, but always a Low Mass accompanied with pious ditties that have no connection whatever with it—or else, what is still stranger, a priest quietly keeps on with his sermon while the one at the altar goes on with the Sacrifice, and the useless chatterbox only holds his tongue when the bell rings at the elevation.

Did I not formerly hear, in the old village church now destroyed, a *Sub tuum* bawled at the singing of the Gospel; and, in the Basilica, the Vespers of our Blessed Lady sung by the diocesan pilgrimage of the place and arranged thus: two Psalms instead of five; for the Hymn the *Ave maris stella* with the first verse sung as a chorus to the rest, and the *Magninificat*; and not a single Antiphon from beginning to end! It were better not to sing Vespers at all than to cut them down in this fashion. As for Saints' Days and the Ferias, here they have nothing to do with them. Generally they celebrate the Office of the Apparition, which at Lourdes takes precedence over the Proper of the Season and over that of the greater part of the Common of Saints; but the Office of our Lady, which was framed by the Benedictines of Solesmes, is superb, and it were ill on my part to make any complaint of having heard it so often.

I recall these splendid Vespers sung on certain Sundays, and I come to regret that they are not always sung in place of those other Vespers that have been so cut down as to be nothing of the kind.

On those Sundays . . . but then there was not this astounding mob of international pilgrimages. The Office was sung in the Basilica: the Antiphons and the Psalms in true plainchant were sung by two choirs, one in the nave, the other behind the altar. The one in the nave was made up from the pensionnat of the Sisters of Nevers—an army of tiny girls in grey hoods edged with blue gimp, expertly trained in plainchant by the Sisters; the other, behind the altar, consisted of the choir-boys and a few choir men, very well trained by the Abbé Darros, the choir-master, and they sang the verses of the Psalms antiphonally, and the hymn *Omnis expertem* all together in a popular melody, but the wonder of the Vespers was the *Magnificat.*

After the Antiphon all the children were silent; and then, from the top of the great organs, over the great doorway, a cry, which was hard and vibrant, burst out like a flame and shook the church—*Magnificat!*

And a band of mountaineers sustained the cry, flung forth far and wide beneath the arches, with the thunder of their voices of bronze. It was full of harshness and violence, but also of a solemnity to take your breath away, of a glory never heard elsewhere! Nowhere was there ever a more majestic storm of praise in honour of the Virgin, and it seemed as if nowhere else had the triumphant gladness of the *Magnificat* been so finely expressed as these fiery Vespers at Lourdes!

The ill-favour of the paltry church vanished; the church, too, was lost in a haze of pearly clouds of incense-fumes and trembled beneath the maze of sunbeams streaming through the window-panes and mixing with the glow of the electric lights burning in the hundreds of bulbs of the chandeliers. One might fancy one was elsewhere, and for a few minutes relish a blissful forgetfulness of Ugliness and the joy of seeing our Lady offered a gift truly worthy of herself.

And I dream of all that could be so lovingly presented to her at Lourdes . . . High Masses celebrated in the Gregorian mode, as is intended, indeed, by the Pope's[1] *Motu Proprio*; the greater and lesser Hours, of which, in public at any rate, one sees no sign in the Basilica and in the Rosary—no one has ever heard the wonderful Office of Compline sung there, even on Sunday. And the Little Office of our Lady which was made expressly for Her, was it not, with its touching and naïve sequences, entirely designated for the purpose of venerating her sorrows and her joys? In short, the *Laus Perennis* of the Marian Liturgy ought to be established at Lourdes. It does go on up to a given point, if you like, since day and night hymns never stop. But what a petty *Laus*, what trashy stuff it is! It is a sort of pious version of "When Johnny comes marching home again" or of "See, the conquering hero comes"; and who can speak of the haunting importunity of the *Ave Maria*, the *Laudate Mariam*, the *Nous vouls Dieu, c'est notre Père*,[2] the *Au ciel, nous la verrons, un jour*,[3] constantly bawled at the top of people's voices in cheap melodies which would find their proper place amongst the rowdies of an East End crowd? And this is what we have to eat and drink here; we go to bed and get up in the morning with it in our ears; it is the very atmosphere of the place, the very wind that blows through Lourdes.

In this town—why not acknowledge it?—the clergy come of a race of mountaineers; they are excellent men, but dead to all that does not belong to the great work of arranging processions and sermons, and to the

---

1 Pius X.
2 "We want God—He is our Father."
3 "In heaven we shall see her someday."

management of crowds. It is also only fair to say that these priests who have taken the place of the Fathers of the Grotto, now driven from their community house, are overwhelmed with work and driven to death with confessions, and one cannot reasonably expect them also to carry out the canonical Offices in their churches—only the Benedictines, if they were installed at Lourdes, could secure such services. And then, if *per impossible* it be admitted that there still remains some sense of the Liturgy in this country, nevertheless it may not—and how likely that is!—in the dioceses of France and of foreign lands which betake themselves to the Grotto—and it would be unseemly enough to ask them to give up their routine and to sing Latin hymns instead of their rigadoons . . . and so no sort of ensemble is practicable.

But, nevertheless, it would not cost the clergy any more if they were themselves to have plainchant at their Offices and to follow to some extent, so far as they could manage it along with their other occupations, the rules of the Liturgy. . . .

Alas! I fear that this aspiration may be as utterly useless as the rest, for, Vespers at the Basilica excepted, the Liturgy and the chant, like the architecture, the painting and the statuary in this place, are all of a piece; in this matter, indeed, they provide an ensemble.

Ah! when the Devil turns pietist, what a dreadful fellow he is!

VIII

LIFE at Lourdes, it must be confessed, is lived L in an amazing spiritual temperature; it is the hotbed of piety. These uninterrupted roarings of the *Ave*, these eddies of the crowd constantly beneath one's eyes, this permanent spectacle of those who suffer and of those who make merry and eat and drink on the grass, as they do on a Sunday at Clamart, end in bewildering one. You live in a milieu destitute of all proportion, in the extreme of sorrow and in the extreme of joy—that sums up Lourdes. After a fortnight of this regime, you are all right; you no longer clash with your surroundings; rather do you unconsciously help to develop them, and the first effect of your self-surrender is an entire lack of interest in all that is taking place in the rest of the world. Nations may exterminate one another and the President may perish, never mind. Lourdes alone exists; newspapers are of no use at all, and you never buy one; all the papers are supplanted by one they sell on the Esplanade, the *Journal de la Grotte*; the important thing is to find out how many miracles happened yesterday, and, apart from that, nothing else matters.

A note from the Record Office, inserted in that very *Journal,* warns the public that the announcements of cures are premature and unverified. Such cautions are not accepted by a single reader; everyone who enters Dr. Boissarie's room or leaves it must have been miraculously healed; the priests are even more rabid than anyone else in their desire to discover miracles on all sides; I have seen some of them fling themselves upon women, who were being carried out from the medical clinic and supposed to be cured, to get them to touch their rosaries, and these women were mere cases of hysteria! How can you make anything out of such a mentality as this? And rumours fly about, originating no one knows whence, that extraordinary prodigies have happened which there has been no time to verify, for they occurred just when the pilgrimages were on the point of going away; and the details grow more and more astounding in proportion as they are told by fresh narrators; the barriers of sound sense which the clinic endeavours to set up against such aberrations are quickly broken down; people think that Dr. Boissarie is guilty of ill-will when he refuses to accept out of hand the miraculous origin of a cure; it is a real rout of all reason!

Furthermore, how strange a world is that which bustles about here! The men are, as a rule, better than those who occupy the churchwardens' pews in churches. There are, indeed, here and there sebaceous faces hollowed out for eyes that twist furtively behind spectacles, but there is also a younger, intelligent-looking generation, especially among the stretcher-bearers; and then there are those of riper years, with none of the sneaking awkwardness of bigots, but whose piety is both simple and strong and truly touching; and then the women!

Among these are some impossible bigots from the provinces; they wander round and jabber, rattling their rosaries just as mules do their curb-chains; they vie with one another as to who will say most, as to who will swill the largest quantity of water, as to who will oftenest make the Stations of the Cross. Devotees, the dreadful set so well known in the chapels of Paris, become quite fearsome females at Lourdes. They have been let loose since yesterday evening. They see a bishop of thirty years of age, with long and dirty hair falling down his back, a Christ-like beard, and hands tattooed in blue, like a wrestler's; and they rush after him, shouting; "How lovely he is! He is the Christ himself!" And when a rumour goes round that he comes from the Holy Land, delirium reigns!

Any other pontiffs they were lying in wait for, to get their rosaries blessed or in order to kiss an episcopal ring, now go for nothing; this exotic product, with his indolent and sickly air, casts them all into the shade; and harassed by the women, he blesses them as much as they wish, offers them his bonbon of an amethyst to suck, and is visibly delighted with the hit he has made. Who can this violet-garbed gypsy really be? for I fancy his confreres regard him with distrust. He is a bishop from Palestine, who has come to France to get money for his priests and to "touch" the faithful with the help of collecting-boxes.

114

And this is the sort of thing I hear around me: "Where does he say Mass? How I wish I could receive Holy Communion at his hands!" What a conception of Catholicism fills these fatuous heads; they imagine that communion given by a young Oriental must be something higher than that administered by a simple priest!

And once having been blessed and reblessed by his obliging Lordship, they indefatigably besiege the spring and toss off cup after cup of water; and then they begin to file through the Grotto and touch the rock where people kiss it beneath the statue, not only with their rosaries and medals, but even with trinkets that have nothing to do with worship, such as cigar-holders, which one of them rubs on the crassly greasy surface of the stone, doubtless in order to sanctify the lips of her fortunate husband! Others stop in front of the wire netting and leave letters there, properly stamped, I like to fancy, for an answer, so that the Virgin may pay attention to them.

Evidently, at Lourdes we reach the very lowest depths of devotion!

This sort of mummery is certainly recruited from the most unintelligent stratum of the people, but I know not whether I do not prefer these edifying geese to the pretentious pietists of a higher grade, springing from the richer middle classes; for some of these are possessed with a desire for making a splash, for getting noticed, for an ostentatious fervour, which ends in becoming intolerable.

You may find them here, dragging along on their knees and looking all about them, telling their rosaries with their arms out in the form of a cross, and kissing the ground. This is quite natural and, indeed, very good when it is done by some simple person who strikes you as being truly recollected and really devout; but when those who perform these exercises have their faces made up with paste and their hair dyed yellow, when they are decorated with jewels and clothed in startling dresses, it rings false. A peasant-woman could pray in those ways and yet not appear ridiculous, but that is not the case when those signs of devotion are accompanied with these amazing exteriors!

I have not seen anyone of this kind among the wonderful infirmarians who look after and bathe the sick. Here, it is always befitting to remember the self-denial and self-sacrifice of these women in order not to be too much roused to indignation against the feminine tribe that frequents Lourdes.

Today there will be over eight hundred sick to be blessed at the time of the procession. I shall follow the cortege behind the Blessed Sacrament. Usually I occupy a place in the front of the organ gallery of the Rosary. In it there are two diamond-shaped openings of daylight in the windows, from which I can take in the whole sweep of the Esplanade. You dominate the scene, and if a sick person gets up with a sudden spring, you watch the running forward of the stretcher-bearers from all sides to surround and protect him against the madness of the crowd, which would tear his clothes off his back to make relics of them. Today I want to see, not only the whole, but the details of the procession, and I betake myself at three o'clock to the Hospitality Association, the president of which is waiting for me in his office: it is situated beside that of Dr. Boissarie, beneath the arches of the terrace that leads up to the Basilica. And there, in a room which also is like a ship's cabin, you will find the power that sets the whole enormous machine of Lourdes in motion. M. Christophe holds the tiller and steers the ship across the reefs of the crowds. He gets the stretcher-bearers ready to move, ensures hospital assistance and shelters, and sees about the arrival and departure of the sick by train; you may well surmise that, during these times of international pilgrimages, his post is no sinecure. I have often asked myself how, amidst the tumult in his office, invaded by directors of pilgrimages, by hospital folk and curés, he does not lose his bearings but answers everybody with patience and a smile; when I get there, he is finishing giving out his orders, and he slips on his litter-braces; and here we are both outside.

We run into the head of the cortege which is being formed and into a packed crowd of onlookers which throngs the broad walks along the Gave. They give way to us, and we reach the Grotto whence the procession is to start.

The Blessed Sacrament, brought from the Rosary, is placed on the portable altar, and it glitters in the furnace of wax-lights. The bishops are already there, from Avignon, Angouléme and Aire, and the long-haired young man from Palestine, and also dignitaries, canons, rigged up in tippets and petticoats, half-violet, half-purple; Capuchins in brown drugget; priests, some in surplices, others in golden chasubles, are waiting behind their Lordships, who are joined by the Benedictine Bishop of Metz, whose violet garb turning to rose-tint reminds me of the altogether rose-tinted taffetas costume with which was clothed, like some frail Cydalise, a Portuguese Bishop of Macao, whom I beheld last year at Lourdes.

Thousands of ecclesiastics and thousands of lay folk, holding candles, extend from the Grotto to the Esplanade, all along the Gave, in two rows preceded by the cross, some choir-boys, and vergers from the Basilica bedizened with silver on a blue background.

In the middle of the procession, which they appear to cut into two halves, before some flying banners, two other beadles, two lanky guys brought from no one knows what diocese—from Nantes, I believe—are dressed up in vermilion and gold, wearing gigantic two-cornered hats surmounted with enormous white catafalque plumes.

We wait for the sign to start; kneeling priests are praying before the Blessed Sacrament; I light the wax-candle given me; laymen run on express messages to and fro between the Esplanade and the Grotto; incredibly self-important gentlemen play the part of police officers, bustling the priests and hustling the pilgrims. What astonishing fellows they are! for did I not once hear one of them, when Mass was being said at the Grotto, say to the crowd: "We are going to give Holy Communion"—that *we* contains a world in itself!

Presently, in front of the monstrance, one of them, waving his white umbrella in his hand, is apparently pointing out to Jesus Christ those of the sick whom he ought to heal, while another makes a gesture, which is quite useless, since it is addressed to Catholics, to kneel down before the Blessed Sacrament when it comes to them.

At last, with the concurrence of such sacrists as these, the procession sets in motion; I follow the bishops, and, behind me, the troop of stretcher-bearers brings up the rear. They sing an amalgam of Latin and French, a pot-pourri made up of the *Magnificat*, alternating verse by verse with this quatrain:

> "Virgin, our hope and expectation,
> Us under thy protection take;
> O save our France, thy chosen nation,
> And never us, thy sons, forsake" (*bis*).

We move slowly forward through a narrow passage in the crowd, and when, after following along the bank of the river, we come out upon the Esplanade, the multitude is like a wall, a sea of heads as closely packed as a flock of sheep farther than we can see; the balustrade, the stairs, the terrace above the Rosary, the broad walks, and the open area in front of the Basilica swarm with people. There is a shoal of white caps, broken here and there with the fiery splashes of bright red parasols; the hill of the Stations of the Cross is closely covered, and its zigzag paths overflow; nothing moves either upwards or downwards, but all huddle together just where they are; never was there such a throng of pilgrims and spectators. Cameras are hoisted a-top of ladders at the foot of the terrace.

The immense circle of the Esplanade, into the hollow of which we are about to make our way, is restricted and formed by a hedge of ambulances of the bedridden who are put in the front row; behind these, on benches, are packed the sick who are still well enough to be seated and the female sick attendants who have to look after them; while farther away, until beyond one's range of vision, the public is accumulated in one compact mass.

The procession ahead of us has now left us for the blessing of the sick; after traversing the whole of the Esplanade, it reaches the Rosary, and there, in the open space before it, it forms up in serried columns. Against the closed doors, beneath Maniglier's bas-relief, rise the banners of nacarat velvet and white silk, embroidered with gold. From one side of the façade to the other stretches a great line, white above and black below— the line of priests in surplices covering their soutanes down to the knee.

In the burning bush of wax-lights, a sprig of which is held by everyone, all the ecclesiastics gather together, and before them, on the edge of the steps, is the troop of choir-boys dressed in the Virgin's blue livery, and there are the beadles in their azure and silver and red and gold uniforms.

And in the background of this picture, standing dead still for a while, I see that certain movements are proceeding. First there is a touch of brown, the peat-coloured costumes of the Capuchins being sent forward, and then a sudden outbreak of violet and purple, the vestments of the canons, separating from the black and white eddies of priests and ranged in the forefront.

The Bishop of Avignon holds the monstrance under an umbrella, surrounded with priests in chasubles and candle-bearers carrying lanterns with the light streaming through their crimson panes.

After him we begin to follow along the hedge of sick folk, and now our hearts are gripped. Oh, these faces that fluctuate betwixt hope and anguish, faces upset from that moment! Some are weeping noiselessly with heads bent down; others, however, look above with eyes drowned in tears; and voices are choking, voices at their last breath; and voices dead already are trying to utter the living shout of invocations, flung forth, with all the power of his lungs, by a priest who has taken his stand alone on the Esplanade:

> "Lord, he whom thou loves the sick!
> Lord, if thou wilt, thou canst cure me!"

And arms are outstretched towards the monstrance, trembling lips stammer, hands are clasped, and afterwards fall clown in despair.

The Blessed Sacrament passes on.

The body of a woman, with her head in her streaming hands, jerks spasmodically.

And nothing moves: the bedridden lie at full length as they are.

And now I again catch sight of my poor unknown friends from the hospital. Amidst the band of the sick from Holland, with their eyes bathed in tears amidst faces like ripe whitlows, or else extremely pallid, the little gnome is buried in rugs beneath his tiny ambulance; his features are set, and his spindle arms and legs are stiff and rigid. He is either asleep or has fainted. And here is the urchin from Belley with his leg fast bound in its wooden gutter. The blue-garbed Sister along with him is bowed in worship beneath her hennin and running through her rosary beads: and he is looking on with a strange air, without emotion.

And the Blessed Sacrament passes on.

Three times they sing the *Monstra te esse Matrem*, which the crowd takes up till it re-echoes long and loud and is repeated far above us by the pilgrims on the hill of the Stations of the Cross.

And still nothing moves.

This field of sickness just traversed, this harvest, bending under a downpour of ills, seems to me, alas! lost in ruin. We have done half our journey and have now reached the steps of the Rosary without a single impotent person having been raised by any breath from on high.

There, on their stretchers, lie the serious cases. A man with a face like a withered leaf opens his eyes; two embers, suddenly lit up, blaze beneath his ashen eyelids. He fixes his gaze eagerly upon the monstrance, and then all is dark: his face, illumined for a moment, becomes once more a shadow. The woman with Pott's disease, bathed in her own suppuration, does not even open her eyes, but looks as if she had already passed out of this world. Farther on, I come across the little White Sister Justinian, who appears to be dead, lying in her basket as if it were a coffin.

How the sight of her smites me to the heart; I cannot tell, but I believe that she will get up, that at last Heaven will answer our prayers. . . .

The Blessed Sacrament, with its golden flash enfolds her beneath the sign of the cross. There she lies, motionless and livid . . .

The priest hurries on with his invocations; the crowd follows after him with a long, low rumble:

"Lord, make me see!
Lord, make me hear!
Lord, help me to walk!"

Then begins the *Adoremus in aeternum*—and still nothing happens. We have filed past the front of the Rosary and are now going back on the left through the avenue which we ascended on our right.

In a harsh voice, growing still more rasping, the implorer shouts:

"Kneel down, throw out your arms, all of you!"

And the huge crowd obeys; prayers pour forth hurriedly, and not a single sick person rises!

Terrible diseases file past us. I thought I had seen all there was to see at the hospital. Unfortunately, there are knots of hydrocephaloid and choreoid cases—a man agitated with trembling paralysis, whose head Jerks hither and thither, shaken like a bell-clapper, and his clutching fingers appear to be trying to unbutton his waistcoat; and, above all, there are dreadful creatures coming from no one knows where, an old man with a calf's muzzle of chewed sticky stuff crusted over; a woman with a nose like a tapir's, the onward drag of which thrusts her eye to the fore, protruding with a white ball on the top of a pedicel; and behind the ambulances there are faces of scorched flesh and others of dead meat, turning green; all these are an overflow from the St Louis Hospital, a chamber of horrors.

The priest goes on with the invocations unweariedly:

"Lord, speak but the word, and I shall be healed!"

Then the *Parce Domine* is sung three times, and flinging his hands heavenwards, with a desperate cry the priest shouts:

"Lord, save us, we perish!"

And the cry, repeated by thousands of voices, rolls down the valley!

The Blessed Sacrament still passes on, and nothing stirs.

At last temptation grips you; reproaches are on the point of breaking from your lips. What can She be doing when it would be so easy for her to cure all these people? After all, in spite of whatever might scandalize her, here there is so much faith, so many prayers, such charity and endeavour—what more can she expect?

The open space in which the suppliant is roaring out his appeals is, nevertheless, not empty. Jesus Christ, Mary and the Angels are there invisible and watching, silent and listening. Jesus has given this definite promise: "Where there are two or three gathered together in my name, there am I in the midst of them." And here we are gathered together in thousands to pray to him! Why does he not answer us? And then suddenly I see before me an old Bruges picture of the Last Judgement by Jan Provost, an early Flemish master, in which Jesus Christ, surrounded with a host of angels, stands out terrible, sword in hand, and with his other hand points to the wound in his heart for the Virgin to see, while she begs him on her knees to spare sinners; and she replies to his gesture of wrath by revealing her breast that gave him suck, confronting with her own bosom his breast transfixed by men.

Is not that what she should do now? And yet not a single stretcher-case is relieved. Here, a Woman in distraction puts forward a child whose eyes are sinking in a decomposing face, and drops down on her knees sobbing; there, a poor man is kneeling, hat in hand, seeming to beg an alms of God, and, as with the rest, God passes on and gives nothing!

It is really dreadful!

The implorer strains to the utmost and roars:

"Thou art the Christ, the Son of the living God!"

And he uses up all the strength he has left in the great shout which is often followed by the swift occurrence of a miracle.

"Hosanna to the Son of David!"

The crowd, with arms outstretched, furiously flings the triumphant cry heavenward, feeling that it is staking its all.

And the Blessed Sacrament continues its progress, indifferent and insensible.

I am discouraged and have no further desire to pray. Nevertheless, I implore the healing of the poor creature with the puffy skin like shagreened leather of the hue of wine-lees: there he is, furtively gleaning his Paternosters and hiding his miserable face beneath the hood of his ambulance.

The procession has returned to its point of departure; all the sick have received a benediction; we turn right about-face, and, traversing the middle of the open space, move in a straight line towards the Rosary.

We begin once more the *Adoremus in aeternum*, repeat the *Monstra te esse Matrem*, and the Bishop of Avignon reaches the approach of the church; he goes in beneath the golden dais prepared for him and presents the monstrance with its shining frame to those before him. The *Tantum ergo* is sung, and, in the great silence of the whole Esplanade prostrate in adoration, he raises the monstrance on high and makes the gleaming sign of the golden cross over thousands of heads.

All is over. People go to fetch carriages and litters and to gather together the bundles of human debris and to take them back to the hospital.

Well, after all, I cannot help thinking of the poor wretches who have come so far, who have undergone such tiring railway journeys, and have not been cured! They are on their way back to their gloomy wards, returning to their beds exhausted after having been shifted about on stretchers and ambulances. And yet I tell myself in an undertone that what we are asking the

Virgin to do here is just folly! Lourdes, in a way, has become a kind of contrary to Mysticism, for, after all, we ought not to be praying at the Grotto for the healing of our ills, but for their increase; there we should be offering ourselves as holocausts in expiation of the sins of all men!

Hence, from that point of view, Lourdes should be considered as the centre of man's cowardice coming here to notify the Virgin of his refusal to accept St Paul's *adimpleo quae desunt passionum Christi*; and then we should be astonished if any cures were wrought by our Lady!

But, first of all, apart from the special vocation of becoming a victim of reparation not being given to everyone, many, when once they are at Lourdes, forget themselves, and beg that others who are worse than themselves may be healed in their stead; and many, as we know, determine to keep their own afflictions for the sake of securing conversions. In this army of stretcher-cases, purified by suffering, there are depths of charity unknown: and how many of them want to be well less for their own sake than for the sake of others—mothers for the sake of their children, maidens for the sake of entering a convent in the service of God, nuns to get back to their charge as infirmarians!

How many, too, there are whose propitiatory role is ended, and so their Mother delivers them! And others, not healed one year, are cured the next, when their time of expiation is over; others, after getting nothing at Lourdes, are unburdened on returning to Paris, like Mlle. Glaser at Notre-Dame des Victoires, or at home, like Marie-Louise Mouchel of Yvetot, who, in 1904, left Lourdes in the same condition as she reached it, with a suppurating sore caused by an operation for appendicitis, and woke up in her room one morning perfectly cured; like Louise Lecuyer, who had coxalgia in her right hip, and regained health in September, 1902, on re-entering her hospital at Pont-de-Veyle; like so many others, who have finally been freed from their maladies on returning home.

Hence there is never any reason for despair, since the miracle often occurs after all expectation of it has been given up.

In any case, people do not agree to undergo the tortures of the journey to Lourdes in vain. You might think that those who leave it in the same state as when they arrived are overwhelmed with despair. That very rarely happens, for if there is no bodily relief, the Virgin almost always grants patience and resignation for the endurance of diseases. The expedition pays for itself in one way if it does not in another.

We want to reason things out, and our poor understanding is so limited! We wish to see nothing but the palpable and the visible at Lourdes! At this very moment, when I am tempted to reproach our Lady with leaving so many sick uncured, she is certainly busied with each one of them, acting for the best in each case, knowing that if such and such a one becomes well he would lose all he had gained from his suffering by the follies he would commit—and in many cases she saves the soul to the detriment of the body, which, even if it recovered its health, must hereafter fall ill, were it but once more only, in order to die.

Lastly, on the Catalaunian fields of earth and heaven, on the battlefield where no slain but only the wounded are to be seen, in that fight which we wage by prayer with God who resists us, and, for reasons we cannot tell, refuses to yield to our petitions, what would become of the merit of believing, if we had nothing but successes to count upon?

Such are the thoughts I ruminate over as I follow the ambulances wending their way in a string through the broad walks towards the Avenue de la Grotte and the hospital; and I pull myself together, feeling that I must relax my nerves and escape from the depression which, in spite of all, lies heavy upon me. I am going to sit at a table on the terrace of the Royal Hotel, where Spaniards, Belgians, and Dutchmen have already gathered into groups. Each country there lives its own life over again in its own way. The Spanish priests smoke cigarettes, laugh with their countrywomen, who fan themselves as they smile on the crowd, tasting ices or drinking chocolate, separated by a band of Belgians quaffing their beer and smoking cigars from the little gathering of Dutchmen taking tea or sampling an appetizer, a Schiedam, while these, too, are smoking cigars.

This reminds me of the little quarters of the Exhibition,[1] the huts to which each individual brings his own customs with him, and plants down in France a compendium of his own country and a miniature of its manners. Here is a Netherlands on a small scale enclosed within its few islands of tables and separated

1 At Paris, 1900.

from the crowd flocking on the roadway by the mole of the footpath; the women with gold headgear, who attracted visitors from the Champ de Mars, are here represented by two magnificent specimens, not barmaids but rich farmers' wives from the Zuyder Zee, present in full dress with their headgear and golden corkscrews and fine lace. No one bothers about anyone else, and everyone is at home at Lourdes; the Dutch unharness; there are the directors of their pilgrimage, the honorary papal chamberlains with their purple sashes, and nothing is more charming than the bonhomie of these old white-haired priests, with their clear eyes and little mouths wrinkled up to discharge a whirl of blue smoke from their cigars; in a fatherly way they joke with the young Dutch girls wearing white bonnets and adorned with marigold yellow ribbons, along with their mothers who are preparing tea, and stop pouring it out to laugh more freely. Young priests, close-knit and with limpidly clear faces, make a circle round their rectors and their flocks, and sip gin as they smoke. You surmise that there is a placidity of spirit, an absence of nerve-storms, amongst these clergy who live like their people and are not a caste apart, a class of outsiders knowing nothing of life itself, like our own clergy who are kept under by the timorous education of our seminaries. All the Dutch pastors seem delighted to wear their soutanes openly, for they can only wear them in Holland, as in any other Protestant country, when at home.[1]

---

1 When Huysmans wrote, most French Catholics believed that no Catholic priest could venture to wear a soutane in public in any Protestant country.

At first sight one might think that these fellow countrymen of St Lydwine are somewhat lacking in asceticism, but then you remember that these ecclesiastics, from daybreak and after, have been toiling as if they were regular porters and waggoners. There are hardly any laymen in their pilgrimage, so they have to act as stretcher-bearers and bath attendants; all have their leather straps on their backs; they are utterly played out, and it is only right that they should now rest and take their amusement before resuming their pious burden tomorrow. With all due deference to one of the strait-laced devotees, who complained to me of their ways, I like this free and easy way very much indeed; a freedom that well befits those who regard themselves as children from a distance paying a visit to their Mother. She, indeed, receives them as a mother, dispensing them from all formality, entertaining them comfortably and indulging them. With her they are at home; and what can be more simple and natural? And then, this sitting at the café tables and quaffing of cordials really do one good; I feel it myself, too, though I have not been drudging as they have. I am tired of sores and prayers and shouts; ambulances are still passing by with the sick, and I refuse to go on looking at them. At most I am stirred by the sorrowful sight of a tall young girl who is being taken from her carriage in front of the hotel and carried in men's arms to the lift to be sent up to her room. She is so utterly undone and so pale that she moves one to tears of pity! But no, I turn my eyes away and will not look; I have done all I could for these poor people; I have begged for their healing; I now beg mercy for myself, too, until tomorrow.

The spectacle to be seen from the terrace is more entertaining and varied than that which can be viewed from any café on the boulevards; Lourdes, in all its cosmopolitanism, files past you, and you do not hear a word of French. Waves from the crowds overflow from the street on to the pavements. The tramway station is opposite the hotel, and the trams run past with a metallic sound, unceasingly blowing their horns to clear the rails; a telegraph-office, temporarily erected close by, is full of invaders: there is a perpetual coming and going of those who are entering and leaving it. All around us floats an odour of dust and vanilla; mountaineers infect Lourdes from morning till night, carrying round packets of old pods, the juices of which have been exhausted by confectioners and scent-manufacturers and then fallaciously revived with a few drops of spirit; hawkers of sheep-skins and carpets and furs, lacking nothing but the Algerian fezzes worn by the Jews of the Rue de Rivoli, slip in between the café tables and try to work off their goods on the women, and, amidst the hubbub of tongues with which the Pyrenean patois mingles, your eardrums split by the strident tones of a flute played by a man bringing in a flock of goats and selling hot milk by the cup.

Street-urchins run along shouting: "*Le Journal de la Grotte!* The latest miracles!" Bold-eyed little girls try to wheedle passers-by out of halfpence; nuns file past with downcast eyes, saying their rosaries; priests from the country cast sidelong glances at priests from abroad who are smoking; and now a tram is on its way down, crammed with women. They are the first party of Spaniards leaving, now on their road to the railway-station, and they bellow vivats, roar like wild beasts, and wave their handkerchiefs. The other Spanish women, sitting in the café and staying on at Lourdes till next day, return their greeting; and the young Dutchwomen, to whom they throw kisses, stand up and wave their hands to them, wishing them a pleasant journey. It is an exchange of courtesies, a mutual bidding of "Good night" on both sides; complete fraternity is established, without anyone noticing it, in this little circle which has perhaps not yet engaged in conversational intercourse.

The Virgin's mantle covers everything, just as in those very old pictures of "The Madonna as Protectress," in which Mary stands up very tall and straight and stretches a large ermine cloak, held up by two holy women, over diminutive figures of all classes and coun-tries and ranks who are praying on her right and left, forming but a single flock sheltered beneath one and the same awning.

IX

WELL, I was accusing the Virgin of not curing the sick in whom I took a special interest, but this morning I have a real joy. I go to the clinic and see the door beset by the crowd. I know the meaning of this swarm of pilgrims. They have just brought Dr. Boissarie one or more cases of cures, or supposed cures, after they have been dipped in the piscinas. Indeed, it is now bathing-time. A stretcher-bearer who knows me clears the way for me, and I go into the office.

"Well, you are just in time," exclaims the doctor. "Now, Sister, you tell him what you felt on being plunged into the water."

I get a thorough shock. Is it possible? The little White Sister from St Brieuc is sitting on a chair with fever-flushed cheeks and eyes, now seen open for the first time, burning like two blue flames. On the ground lies her wicker basket, a deranged appliance, some bits of plaster and linen bandages spotted with recent discharges.

In a panting voice, Sister Justinian says joyously and rapidly: "Yes, I did, indeed, suffer; the whole of my right hip snapped; they took me out of the water, but as I was still in pain I asked to be put back, and then the pain went away. I felt that my right leg had become straight, and got up."

"And how long were you held fast in your appliance?" asks the doctor, while he verifies the wording of the medical certificates in his hand.

"One year, but I had been kept in bed a long time before I was put in plaster." And then she adds, speaking to herself: "How pleased our Mother will be!"

"You will have to go back to the piscina before you leave us," observes the doctor. "Your hip has regained its suppleness, but that is not the case with your knee. Now try to walk a little."

The Sister stands up and takes a few steps, but with difficulty. They bring her a chair, and, while the tumult in the crowd outside the door and windows is growing, Dr. Boissarie cries out:" They will pull her to pieces when she goes out!" And he orders the stretcher-bearers to get her a carriage and to go with her. "No," he replies, "you had better leave by the back-door"—but it, too, is blocked by a crowd which wants to see the Sister. After the stretcher-bearers have left the room, we have to buttress the door with our shoulders in order to shut it.

"Do you know," the doctor asks me, "that the little fellow belonging to the Belley pilgrimage is on his feet?"

"The one with the wooden splint?"

"Yes."

Well, indeed, I must go and myself verify his condition. I fling myself head downwards into the throng;

but at every step I am pulled up by women asking questions about the malady of the sick nun who has been miraculously healed. A priest who is unknown to me is ready to fly into a rage when I tell him that the cure cannot be definitely vouched for, since the knee is still swollen; I am sure he looks upon me as an infidel. At last I manage to get clear of the hustle, and on my way I reflect that, short of a complete cure which will doubtless be only the matter of a few days, the little nun has been so divinely changed as to be now unrecognisable. She who was so powerless to move, so livid, so weak, so seemingly dead, is now to be seen talking in her chair with burning eyes and flushed cheeks! I felt as if I were in the presence of one raised from the dead. Will it be the same with the little urchin?

Once at the hospital, I climb up to the room set apart for the pilgrims from Belley, and the first thing I see is the wooden splint lying empty on the bed; and the good Sister in her hennin joyously claps her hands on seeing me.

"Don't you think the Blessed Virgin is spoiling us? We have already two of our sick cured! There is the lady downstairs who could only drink her milk with the help of an India rubber tube; well, now she is not afraid of veal and potatoes! When she has finished one slice, she asks for another! And the little boy you used to come to see—what a miracle he is!"

"Where is he, Sister?"

"Where is he? Why, he is running about the passages; he cannot be kept still. I will fetch him for you."

She goes out and brings him back in a few minutes.

"Just fancy," she says, "we had to buy him some shoes, for he came on a litter without any shoes, and while a good lady went to the shoemaker's, he would not sit still, but galloped down the passages barefooted."

I ask the brat if he is pleased. He says nothing, but surveys his shoes with a vexed expression.

"Come, silly!" says the Sister, "you know well we are going to have them changed, since you want yellow ones; the lady is going to take you today to choose them: and now, don't sulk, but answer the gentleman's questions."

"What did you feel when you were dipped in the water?"

"I don't know." At last, by dint of asking, the Sister gets out of him that he felt a shock, but it did not hurt him.

"Come, turn round, and let me change your shirt while I have got you." And then the Sister takes off his shirt, which still has some spots of fresh matter on it, and I note a ring of dry abscesses with half lifted crusts on his loins, and beneath them appears an entirely new and thin reddish skin.

"When you think that these abscesses were quite active and discharging a great deal of matter!" says the Sister. "And just look at his leg; it is now straight, and he can use it as well as the other, without effort or fatigue. The urchin will not even limp. He is quite cured."

He gets fidgety and does not conceal his desire to be off. We let him go and away he dashes, as hard as he can, from the room.

"Fancy!" exclaims the Sister. "We had to be rough with him to bathe him; he stormed, as he was so afraid of the water; indeed, he nearly drove us wild, the little rascal!"

I take leave of her and go to say a decade of the rosary in the hospital chapel. There is something very delightful in this little sombre chapel, with a more intimate touch about it than any other in Lourdes; it is like a crypt, with its low vaulted ceiling and its altar in the background amidst the gloom surmounted with a Pietà, while, a little farther on, stands a statue, improved by the dimness, of a saint whose position is here well justified, St John of the Cross bearing a sick man in his arms. While I am saying my prayers some of the patients are murmuring the rosary in their seats; and here the noise of the hospital, with the feverish commotion of its passages, dies in silence.

And once more I think over the differences of mode in the various cures. Sister Justinian suffered a great deal in the piscina; her leg got right again, but her knee remained stiff and swollen; the little boy felt no pain, and was made lissom and well on the spot.

I dwell upon such reflections as these as I leave the hospital, but as soon as I have passed through the railings I run into a fresh pilgrimage which is on its way to the Grotto; and at the head of it walks an automaton brandishing an English flag. All of them, men and women, display tricoloured ribbons in their buttonholes, the colours running up and down in straight lines. None of them are singing, but some spectacled women, with teeth protruding from their gums, are croaking.

A priest I happen to know, an habitué of Lourdes, tells me that these English people will get hold of all they can seize; they will take the best places and insist on being at the head of the processions—"but don't be alarmed, we shall not have to be hampered and bothered with their slap-dash ways very long; the day after tomorrow they will all be off on an excursion; they have brought very few patients or none at all; indeed, they are rather tourists than pilgrims."

We go down to the Esplanade together.

"Consider," continues the priest, "that, despite the quantity of people praying here, there are but few indisputable miracles just now at Lourdes. If you want to know why, perhaps it is because of the crowd of spectators who have motored over from Pau, Bagnères, Argelès, Cauterets, Luchon, and all the watering-places round, to gossip and seek entertainment here out of sheer curiosity."

And while, after talking of the poverty of brain and the wretchedness of soul of the majority of these disastrous snobs rigged up like wild beasts to crush to death, in their delirium for speed, the poor women and children on the road, the conversation turns upon the instigations of Satanism, I quickly come to realise how unappreciative an intelligent priest may be in matters of art. I speak of the monumental ignominy of Lourdes, but he has never noticed it.

"It is just the same as anywhere else," he remarks.

"No, no; it is not just the same: it is worse here in our Lady's dower."

139

"Ah!" he exclaims, when I explain to him the sly triumph of diabolism to be seen in the statues set up in the churches and along the Esplanade "there is something more than that. You know, as well as I do, that the presence of the Virgin induces the presence of the devil; but there is something special of this kind at Lourdes. It might be shown that the devil was the first to take possession of the place, and that our Lady has come to hunt him out of it.

"However far you go back, you will find confirmation of the fact that this place was always a haunt of the Accursed One. Researches into prehistoric times led to the discovery in the Espelugues caverns, near the Grotto, of carved flints, commanders' batons, arrowheads, antlers of reindeer, skeletons of animals, and, above all, of men's bones which had been cloven down the middle to get the marrow out of them. Hence we may infer that human sacrifices abounded here, and that victims were here cut up and roasted and eaten.

"Furthermore, there is a legend about the solid square rock behind the statue of our Lady, in the hollow of the Grotto at the very place where She appeared. According to some, this block of granite shows such a peculiar structure that you would have to go all the way to Mongolia to find a similar specimen. If that is so, it must have been brought there, but at what period and by what nomadic tribes, no one knows. According to others, it is composed of the same material as the dolmens of Brittany. Lastly, some think that the block must have come down from the granite chain of Gavarnie, which formerly extended into the plains of Lourdes.

However that may be, if they are not agreed about the original provenance of it, geologists are of one accord in regarding the block as a sacrificial stone dedicated to infernal divinities who could only be propitiated by constant libations of blood . . ."

While listening to these stories, I tell myself that they prove nothing whatever as to the peculiar diabolism of Lourdes, for stones of that kind and calcined and cloven human bones have been found in most of the caves of all countries.

But my priest runs on: "In a book recently published by the firm of Savaete, Mgr. Goursat quotes the testimony of two archaeologists, MM. de Gaumont and de Mirville, according to whom this stone must have been specially dedicated to Venus Astarte—that is to say, to her whom Eusebius calls the infamous demon, the cruel goddess of Pleasure. And his conclusion is that the Immaculate Conception must have appeared at Lourdes to drive away from the Grotto the cultus of that original sin from which She was exempt.

"Here, you see, we are on almost certain ground; but there is another, and that more unstable, I confess, yet also going a long way back, the ground of pure legend. You know it, don't you? According to a tradition which appears to derive its inspiration from the story of Sodom, Lourdes formerly stood on the edge of a lake stretching to the left of the Bay of Biscay; and to punish this town for its sins, the nature of which the similarity of its chastisement enables you to surmise, God engulfed it, as in a Dead Sea, beneath the waves of the lake. A woman whom he had spared disobeyed him as she fled, and was changed, not into a pillar of salt like Lot's wife, but into a monolith—and this monolith is none other than that of Peyre-Crabere on the Pouyferré road.

"From all these fabulous tales, it seems to follow that this town, now chosen by the Virgin, was one of the devil's most ancient lairs."

"After all, it is quite possible."

Thus was it at Garaison, the prototype of Lourdes, where Mary appeared in the land of the Goat in Satan's own seat amidst the nocturnal debaucheries of the witches' revels; but, not to speak of the latter-day occurrences in the Grotto of Massabielle, the reappearance of the taint of Eden, the infernal cries heard by Bernadette, and the sham visionaries, I believe there are enough actual evidences to prove that diabolism rages in various aspects at Lourdes to dispense one from making sure of the more or less of truth there may be in the fictions retailed to me by my friend the abbé.

We take leave of one another, and he goes towards the Rosary, and I, wishing today to escape from the inundation of the crowd, go for my walk as far as the convent of the dames of the Immaculate Conception, which stands behind the quarters of the old Garaison Fathers and the Bishop's House on the road to Bétharram.

Since the two years in which I have come here, I have indulged in nothing but unflattering thoughts concerning these nuns who are called by the inhabitants of these parts—*les grandes dames, les coquettes de Dieu*—doubtless on account of the richness of their theatrical costume, for they wear long flowing white robes when they go to chapel; but in the street, they are more simply accoutred, to tell the truth, in blue.

In any case, they are extremely businesslike dames and somewhat difficult to deal with. They take ladies *en pension*, which, of course, exasperates the caterers and hotel-keepers of Lourdes, and they are in dispute with their Ordinary about party walls and rights of way. They have lost their suit, but have managed so well at Rome that they have succeeded in getting free from the jurisdiction of the Bishop of Tarbes.

Well, I am quite indifferent about these disputes, and I merely propose to visit their chapel, hoping to find comparative solitude there, so as to be able to say my prayers in peace.

After going along the road, above which open the caves hollowed out in the lower part of the Espelugues hill, whereon is erected the amazing group of the Way of the Cross, and looking at these excavations closed with iron bars and transmuted into damp chapels, one of which is dedicated to Our Lady of the Seven Dolours, while at the bottom of another is to be seen an image of St Mary Magdalene, I come out in front of a luxurious monastery with a tiny church, the first sight of which does not fail to prove somewhat disconcerting. The entrance is a glazed rotunda, a regular conservatory, giving on to a passage also glazed and ending with a swinging door of scarlet velvet; you push it open, and then before you extends a long gallery and a pretentious little drawing-room, with an altar at the far end of it. All the petty devotions, not to be found in other sanctuaries at Lourdes, have taken refuge in this oratory: St Antony of Padua and St Expeditus are represented by painted plaster statues from the Rue Saint-Sulpice, but the pièce de resistance and chef-d'oeuvre is a coloured wax statue of St Philomena lying in a box with a glass lid which opens like a desk for people to slip in their visiting-cards or letters!

And while I am kneeling down somewhat flurried, dames in long white trains make stately entries and exits from the courtyard or the garden into the choir. There is a stagey air about them, and they take a look at the public to see that they are being admired. Oh, these "do-you-see-me's" at their devotions!

Decidedly, this is not the place for calm renewal that I was hoping for; this sort of nun does not incite to prayer, and, as soon as I get into the road again, I think of another queer convent in which no religious in their habits are to be found, but rather fussy women in town dress.

This convent is situated at the other end of the district, at the foot of a stiff bare hill, which looks like a heap of household refuse piled up in bygone ages, and possesses a singular chapel with Turkey red hangings, sown with yellow lilies and decked with Italian ingenuities of godliness, both outrageous and amiable, such as are to be seen in the show-cases of shop-windows in the Rue du Bac at Paris.

In this place there used to be a figure of Christ so constructed as to be able to move its eyes and hypnotise purses into shedding their contents. The bishop intervened and had it done away with. As for myself, whenever I go into this red box which partakes somewhat of the music-hall and somewhat of the travelling-show, I always get the impression of scenting a whiff of heresy. Moreover, no sort of Office is sung in it; the religious—if they are religious—are Passionists, but Passionists of an independent kind, depending on no house of the Order.

Happily, Lourdes includes institutions of a sounder sort: the Dominican nuns lodged on the height behind the railway; the Carmelites opposite the Grotto across the river; and the Poor Clares close to the falls of the Gave.

I walk along in a leisurely way, looking at the flowers by the roadside, which are more striking and perfumed than those that grow in the plains. Here the green hellebores are enormous, the lungworts with rose-tinted or lilac bells and leaves inlaid with white are twice the size of those grown in the centre of France; but, for sumptuousness of colouring, the first place must be given to the rocks. On this road there are rocks splashed with the powdered silver of lichens, while others are richly clothed in mosses of golden yellow and vivid orange.

And every moment I meet women coming back from the forest with heavy bundles of wood poised on their heads. In this country that is the way they carry everything, be the burden heavy or light, faggots or baskets or the tiniest of parcels; the important thing is to have your hands free and to be able to knit as you walk.

And then there are heavy cradle-shaped carts passing, drawn by little bullocks with a sheepskin over their heads and a white cloth round their bodies.

While clambering up and down—for it is almost impossible to find a piece of flat road at Lourdes—I come into a gorge near an unexpected spring and a little bridge. This valley is the vale of chaos. Farther than the eye can see range giant grey peaks, stripped and leafless, and piles of formidable debris, rolled down from above, bestrew the ground. You might think you were thousands of miles away from any inhabited region and where nature runs absolutely wild, but for the telegraph posts placed here and there amidst the ups and downs of the slopes, and the sound of quarrymen's hammers, which tells you that they are gradually quarrying out hollow gaps in the mountain-sides.

I take a seat on the ledge of the little bridge. Oh, the joy of being alone awhile! You sober clown, for really at last you get rather intoxicated with the clatter of crowds; you are no more yourself, but a compound of I know not what frenzied creatures turning round and round upon themselves like teetotums. There is no way of retreat; you cannot see, your soul is sea-sick; all is in a muddle; inward prayer is hardly allowed, for just when you would practise recollection, the rosary is being recited in a loud voice, and you are yourself drawn in by the cogs of the vocal wheel and grind out your prayers along with it.

No—Lourdes is far from being a delightful spot for those who love heart-to-heart intercourse with the Virgin in the silence and dimness of the old cathedrals!

But we must constantly repeat the question: Where is to be found a blossoming of grace and flowering of charity more glorious than here?

And this is something so abnormal at a time when everyone is pursuing but one aim, that of growing rich at his neighbour's expense, that from this point of view Lourdes really presents, in the records of this age, a spectacle which is unique!

At this hour, in which Society is riven in every section of it and splitting up, in which the whole earth is poisoned with the germs of sedition, and uneasily expecting what may be brought forth; at this hour in which beyond the darkness on the horizon the slow tolling of the passing bell can be clearly heard, it seems as if the blazing Grotto of Lourdes had been set there by the Virgin, as a great fire kindled on the mountain, to be a beacon and guide for sinners straying through the darkness that is overspreading the world.

And as I retrace my steps and once more take the road back to the town, far away, instead of the passing bell tolled by the future, I hear, like a gentle protest against the panic of the times now preparing, the hour striking at the Basilica above the Grotto on four notes borrowed from the old sweetly caressing chant of the *Inviolata: O Benigna, O Regina, O Maria!*

X

WHILE such crowds of caravans are floundering about Lourdes, once more the surest refuge is to be found on the Carmelite chapel lodged atop of the hill on the road to Pau and just opposite the Grotto, from which it is separated by the Gave. It is unknown to the pilgrims who pass their time down below in the town or upon the Esplanade. Here no one takes any interest in St Teresa, nor, indeed, in any other saint; only the Virgin exists, and She alone is the subject of the hymns and chants; everyone says the rosary during Mass; the Common and the Proper of the Saints and the Proper of the Season are alike unknown; nowhere is the hyperdulia of our Lady so vehemently accentuated as at Lourdes!

Yet on certain days the Carmelites are invaded; for when the arrival of hundreds of priests is announced, all the altars in all the churches are at once engaged by the hosts of the clergy on the spot, and wooden altars are installed in all the chapels of the monasteries in the town, and to the newcomers are allotted something like tourists' tickets for Mass and lodgings. Ecclesiastics belonging to one pilgrimage are Sent to the Poor Clares, those belonging to another to the Dominican Convent, and so forth. The Carmelites, like the other communities, then give shelter to crews of celebrants. And then the chapel becomes a gallery edged round with tables, at which some of the priests with their noses to the right-hand wall, and the others with their noses to the left-hand wall, stand back to back as they press on with the celebration of the Mass. But when this rapid fire is over, all returns to order; furthermore, in the afternoon, the chapel, being indeed far from the Grotto—for you have to go a long way round to cross the Gave, as there is no bridge—is almost empty.

It is the only place in which—if you don't want to practise recollection in your own room—you can take stock of yourself and pull yourself together; and, after all, how lacking in quiet intimacy is this usually placid shrine! It is something like the hall of a casino in one of the many bathing resorts of the district; it is a collection of glaringly coloured windows and of statues made wholesale, and it is adorned with an altar of the most showy of its kind, and as costly as possible. The hall has an affectation of Gothic about it, and along with such pretensions it displays the crude glaring whiteness of plaster, and the shining woodwork of its seats and flooring, ruthlessly polished, gives you a sharp sense of newness which smites you as soon as you have pushed open an amazing door all of glass; and this, along with the ornamental colouring on a blue background, revives afflicting reminiscences of the stained windows made in medieval style for certain breweries of the

Latin Quarter; it would certainly be much more in its place there than here.

This chapel is attached to an enormous building erected according to the notions of Father Peyramale, the first builder of Lourdes.

Full of the desire to work on a grand scale, this priest took no notice of the rule of St Teresa which only allows a very small number of religious to each convent, and promoted the erection of a colossal barrack, in which regiments might manoeuvre at ease. The holy women who dwell in it are almost lost in its monumental immensity, the upkeep of which overwhelms them. Happily, through the grille which cuts them off from the choir, they cannot see this pompous chapel so ill befitting their Order, which is dedicated by its constitutions to the practice of poverty and to the exercise of penance.

And, nevertheless, if you shut your eyes at high Mass on Sunday, when you hear their wailing chant behind the grille, all the false glitter loses its importunity, and Lourdes, with its everlasting kermesse, and even its vision of the Madonna in triumph, vanish away, and you are reminded of that other apparition of the Virgin which took place twelve years previously, on another mountain-chain that rivals the Pyrenees, to weep and to preach penance, and you suddenly remember that at Lourdes, too, the Immaculate Conception thrice spoke the word "penance" to Bernadette.

But I fancy that these words strike a discordant note in this milieu. Neither the ways of the pilgrims, nor the appearance of the churches, nor the hymns sung by the

150

crowds, nor even the selections from the liturgy which is only joyful in this place, stir people to thoughts of contrition and repentance.

The place itself is decidedly against them. The scenery is the gay landscape of comic opera, with family mountains and children's caverns and peaks *à la papa*; it is not a case of nature on the grand and barren scale of La Salette; you are not looking down into abysses in a region without trees or birds or flowers when you are in a square no larger than the Place Saint-Sulpice, beyond which there are no dreadful ravines; whereas up at La Salette you are alone amidst the clouds with the Virgin, and there are no distractions, no cafés, no newspapers, no panoramas, no excursions in charabancs, and, lastly, no funicular railway to hoist you pleasantly up to the top of the mountain!

There you are thrown back upon yourself, whereas you live a free and open life at Lourdes; there you are really on a pilgrimage of expiation, and I believe it is now quite deserted and abandoned, so little did it respond to the thrills of the crowd!

But the figure of Our Lady of the Seven Dolours, who formerly cured so many sick folk and scattered so many blessings at La Salette, will always be more attractive to certain souls than that of the young blue and white Virgin without Child or Cross at Lourdes. It was the old time-honoured Virgin of the crucifixion who appeared in the Alps, the Mother whose heart was a scabbard for swords. . . . And now she is back once more in this chapel at Lourdes, to which she has been recalled by St Teresa and by the very sadness of the chants providing such a remarkable contrast to the cheerful tunes the hum of which you can hear coming in from outside!

She rolls you flat; you were thinking of Her alone, and it seemed all right—and you think of yourself, and it seems horrible!

The setting of the spectacle outside had laid hold of you with its pity for the sufferings of some, with its vague acquiescence in the coarse merriment of others. You were away from your own soul, which gained such satisfaction as it could amidst the pell-mell of impressions coming from without, amidst the utterance, also external, of vocal prayers; and you never thought of going deep down into your inner dispositions; and here is Mount Carmel waking you out of your torpor, which was delectable after all, for it dispensed you from the toil of repentance and exempted you from the pangs of regret!

But all bitter self-reproach for forgotten deviations vanishes as soon as you leave the Carmelite Convent, for the permanent atmosphere of the cheery crowds recaptures you. At the very door of the cloister the portresses are joyfully talking of the monster procession which is being arranged for tonight, a whole army-corps of thirty thousand pilgrims marching with lighted candles to the Rosary, passing along the steep zigzag paths that make an "M" on the slope of the hill behind the Basilica, and, after descending and ascending the terraces, going through their evolutions on the Esplanade till they finally wind up by converging into a single mass in the immense circle of the Rosary.

While waiting for the torchlight festival of this evening, I once more assist at the four o'clock procession; but now, instead of following the Blessed Sacrament or looking on at the ceremony from the loft-windows of the church, I join in the crowd. In it there are many fervent pilgrims, but also many idle sight-seers from the neighbouring health-resorts, who are walking round the ring of sick folk as if they were a military band in the Tuileries. These are not the people to help us with a contribution of prayers and an increase of grace!

True it is that the spectacle they are about to witness is not calculated to inspire them with respect for a religion they know nothing of.

Almost at the head of the cortege, behind the cross, the candle-bearers and the blue beadles—the red beadles with the hearse-plumes have left with the pilgrimage that brought them—a brass band, which came only yesterday, advances. It is made up of clergy and laity, amongst whom towers a giant in a soutane, blowing into an ophicleide with enough energy to tear out the horns of a buffalo.

They are playing popular tunes of the tol-de-rol type!

And as soon as they come into the sick folk's encampment an unseemly quarrel breaks out with these roughs, who prove refractory as soon as they are asked to be quiet, so that the priest who acts as implorer may begin the invocations!

The Blessed Sacrament makes its way as usual round the ring of ambulances. In front of me there is a swirl of heads; people stand on tiptoe to see; children are astride their fathers' shoulders; ladies climb up on to benches and chairs; the photographers' ladders are invaded. One might suppose that it was a mob on the lookout for the prize ox. Here and there, however, priests are placidly reading their breviaries. And suddenly a thrill passes through the crowd. Cries break forth: a miracle! A woman is getting up! *Magnificat!* I see the stretcher-bearers running as hard as they can into the empty circle. The best thing is to slip through to the clinic as quickly as possible before the general rush comes, so as to be there when the woman is brought in.

On my arrival Dr. Boissarie is talking to a young girl sitting in an arm-chair in front of him.

She is telling him how she had not been cured of her paralysed right hand and arm either in the piscinas or processions during the past week she had been at Lourdes, but this morning, on the Calvary hill, to which she had betaken herself to make the Way of the Cross for the last time before leaving, she was suddenly healed. Her cure had taken place when she had given up expecting it, just when she was about to go away, and was making the sign of the cross at the end of her prayers as she said Amen.

And then the little girl waves her arm in all directions and laughs as she looks with some gratification at a rolled-gold and paste ring which she enjoys moving up and down her finger.

"Come," says the doctor with a smile, "you had not this ring on when your fingers were twisted back inside your hand?"

"Oh no: only when I was cured I was so glad that I ran off at once to buy one!"

And then, fearing she might be blamed for coquetry, she adds with a slight blush: "I have had it blessed!"

Everyone laughs, and I think the little girl is not lacking in a spice of cunning, for after all she has managed to put her conscience under cover and to retain a trump in hand with regard to the Virgin by transforming an article of vanity into an article of piety! Well, she has enough of the woman in her, hasn't she?

The door opens with a puff of wind and in a storm of voices; the office is suddenly full. A litter is hastily shoved through on to the floor ark the stretcher-bearers are struggling behind it, amidst the crush of the crowd. We have to help them to beat back their assailants with all our strength, and to close the door.

The office is more and more like a ship's cabin beaten by a flood of waves, and outside is to be heard the rumbling of the sea on the Esplanade, where swarms the crowd, waiting for the exit of the woman who has been miraculously cured.

"Come," says the doctor, as he looks at the person whom the stretcher-bearers are helping to get up from the litter, "what does all this mean?"

All who have got into the office behind her are talking at once.

"A moment's silence, please, gentlemen!" cries the doctor. "Let the lady tell us all about it."

But she cannot tell us anything; she is bewildered, and confines herself to saying: "I am cured, I am cured!"

"To what pilgrimage do you belong? Have you a medical certificate?"

She knows nothing about it; however, at last we gather that the certificate is at the hospital.

Finally, a priest who knows her declares that hers is an epileptic case of intermittent paralysis.

"Very well," says Dr. Boissarie, "we will look into the case later on."

Then he shrugs his shoulders.

"A poor catch!" say I, in taking leave of him.

He smiles. "Well," he observes, "whatever certain newspapers may say to the contrary, I think you are convinced that here miracles are not made to order."

Just as I am on my way out, the brass band, now let loose, is blaring on the Esplanade. The clodhopper in the soutane with the ophicleide is extracting from it the bellowings of a cow in dire distress, belchings both pious and profound.

There is only one thing to be done, to go home and close one's windows in order, if possible, to escape from the indefatigable shindy of these folk.

About eight o'clock calm once more prevails. The Orpheans, doubtless, are still guttling and guzzling. I shall go back again to my good portresses at the Carmelite Convent, and I sit down beside some priests on the chapel steps. Thence I look down, across the Gave, upon the Basilica, the terrace, the Esplanade, and the Rosary, all seen in profile: it is the best possible place for witnessing the gala of fiery enchantment.

While waiting for the defiling to begin, we talk, and our conversation naturally turns upon the arrivals and departures of pilgrims and upon miracles. They ask if I have been to the clinic today and if I have witnessed any prodigies. I tell the story of the little girl with the ring, who was cured when she was not thinking about it and no longer expecting it; and with regard to this unlooked-for cure, an ecclesiastic, whose face I cannot make out in the dimness, and who, according to a few particulars which he was just now imparting to someone next him, must be a priest of the Holy Face at Tours, exclaims:

"Miracles! M. Dupont once told an onlooker who expressed his astonishment at the cures he was obtaining with the oil of a lamp burning before the Holy Face: 'Why, sir, a Christian can get a miracle just as easily as you can get a dish of peas from the greengrocer round the corner; he only has to ask for them. . . .'

"Only M. Dupont used to ask in a special way. He used to tell God not 'I wish,' but 'I will have.' Once he rebuked a young girl with a bad foot, who spoke to the Lord thus: 'O Lord, if it be thy will, I beg thee to cure me.'

"'That is not the way to pray,' he cried; 'you have no faith, you must address God with a command!' Perhaps that is how we should act when Christ does not yield. . . ."

"Perhaps so," remarked another priest, "for when Père Marie Antoine came to Lourdes, he used to employ that method of impetration, and did it with success."

"Yes, but the old Capuchin was a holy man, and his exclamatory eloquence fired the crowds, and thus he had at his disposal an astonishing power of prayer which he knew how to handle."

And while they are chattering together and reviving their memories of Père Marie Antoine, in the distance and beneath our eyes the procession is forming.

At this hour, amidst the darkness, the Grotto hollowed out beneath the Basilica is blazing like a furnace. Thence it is that the fire starts and is carried onward by the wax-lights of pilgrims unseen by us. It looks as if sparks were flying from an open oven and carried away by the wind, fluttering up the zigzags on the hill, which are slowly breaking into flame; and the flashes gain ground and are already sparkling among the trees behind the apse of the Basilica and gradually coming, as they turn the corner, to the open court in front of it before running down the right-hand terrace, amidst an indescribable cacophony made by the singing of *Laudate Mariam* and *Au ciel, au ciel!* mixed with hymns in foreign languages, yet all overwhelmed by the heavy volume of the *Aves*.

And now the Basilica is alight from top to bottom, and stands forth outlined in red, white and blue amidst the darkness, looking narrower and poorer than ever against the background of mountains which look bigger in the blackness deepened by the streaks of light that slash it through. The round foot warmer with its cover on beneath the feet of the Basilica, the roof of the Rosary, sparkles with its metal dome and its red bull's-eyes. Now both the terraces are fully a flame; it looks like a wheel of fire, lying on its side and partially raised from the ground, turning and crackling as it flings forth, amidst its gyrations, showers of sparks. The ascending wax lights hurry forward and seem to be marching with victorious cries to the assault of the Basilica, when suddenly, amidst the sparkling rows, great holes appear; the wind has blown out the candles, and fireflies are flitting along to set them alight again, and the black holes disappear, stopped up with bundles of flame!

And the wheel turns and turns without ceasing, amidst a din of *Aves* as accompanied by the brass instruments of the band. In the distance the overflowing Esplanade suggests the thought of a plain of crops on fire, in which the ears of corn are a flame; and the stalks of the burning crops fling a sort of theatrical illumination over the surrounding trees, the green of which grows albuminised and discoloured.

Opposite the Grotto, along the Gave, tiny trains are still being formed, and you might think they were swarms of glittering worms winding along the ground, and then changing, as they cast off their chrysalises and flutter upwards along the zigzags on the hill, into golden moths. These wax-lights are singing, but their weak and scarcely audible voices are at last lost in the vastness of the ensemble that imparts its motion to the darkness of the mountains.

How strange is the prospect, how bewildering the spectacle afforded by this crowd from all the nations of the world gathered into this little insignificant corner to invoke the Virgin! A few steps away the country lies silent and dark; and all these people who are watching here, so far from their native lands, say one and the same thing in their different languages and are of one mind: all are sure that patients given up by their doctors can be healed in a moment, if the Virgin wills it; that conversions regarded as impossible and matters inextricably tangled can be wrought or unravelled in a twinkling; and in this innumerable host, without any police control, there is never a disturbance, never a dispute; and even such effervescence as miracles may give rise to subsides of its own accord. In this city of our Lady there is a return to the early ages of Christianity, a flowering of loving care that will last as long as people are beneath her spell in this haven of her own. Here you get an idea of a people made up of various fragments, and yet so united as never any people was; they will be broken up tomorrow by departures, but unity will be restored by the arrival of fresh constituents, brought hither by fresh trains, and nothing will be changed; there will be the same devotion and the same patience and faith. In fine, Lourdes is a principality which realises the wildest dreams of the philanthropists, and far more; here there is the temporary fusion of classes; here the woman of the world dresses the wounds of the working woman and cleans her down; the nobleman and the middle-classes become beasts of burden to the artisan and the rustic, and wait upon them as bath-attendants.

The poor man is lodged and fed, and bathed and nursed for the love of God; he can draw as much water as he likes from the spring; he can take a seat in any of the churches and at the Grotto wherever he likes, without spending a single penny.

The vision of a society as it should be is revealed for a few months every year at Lourdes. It is owing to the virtue that St Paul puts above all others—to that of charity; and I make the melancholy reflection, that if Christ's precepts were followed, existence would smile kindly upon all men; but this is where Utopia begins; for no one feels any solicitude for his neighbour who, indeed, generally tries only to exploit you, and, on the other hand, the infidels have only one aim, to persecute Catholics who are sorry they have no power themselves to persecute the ungodly, forgetting that though they have the right to become martyrs, their own religion forbids them to make any.

And while I am thus ruminating, the fiery wheel keeps on turning, but it is already sending forth fewer sparks, and the more it cools down and darkens the more brightly glows a brazier beneath it in the basin formed by the encircling terraces in front of the Rosary. Thither all the wax-lights have gone down; and when the terraces are altogether dark, and the wheel has stopped revolving, an immense flaming fire breaks forth in the basin.

And then arises a splendid spectacle, never to be forgotten.

The incongruous roars have died away into silence, and from the incandescent basin soars up the *Credo* in plainchant. It is unfurled and upborne with the help of thousands of voices, and rises from amongst the flames with an august lingering movement into the darkness of the sky.

It is the profession of faith of the whole world finally freed from the confusion of tongues to find expression in the language of the liturgy; it is the concentration of the individual prayers of the day now gathered up into a single sheaf of common prayer; it is the offering to the Lord—before whom the Virgin, who has been hitherto set on high, disappears—of the vocal perfume of the Apostles' Creed, of the incense of the chant of his own Church!

And high up yonder, right up in the sky, while the solemn tones of the *Credo* linger in the air, a new constellation rises on the top of the Great Gers, invisible in the gloom, a constellation rutilating in the form of a cross amidst the scramble of the rest of the stars, a cross lit up with electric rays atop of the vanished mountain peak!

It is ended; the burning basin goes out in smoke; the fiery harvest on the Esplanade has been reaped; the procession breaks up and the lights are dead. Alone, the huge hollow of the Grotto goes on flaming. Nevertheless, here and there pearls of light bound off, as from a necklace with a broken thread, and roll away by themselves, parting from one another along the roads. Some candle-ends are glowing towards extinction along the Gave; a few will-o'-the wisps are still fluttering near the Rosary, but they, too, soon disappear in the blackness.

And now all is quite finished; I don't know—but I have the idea that this splendid fiery scene is independent of us and that we go for nothing in it, that what we have seen is an allegory and a figure. The reality, as it seems to me, what is hidden beneath the appearances, is something else.

I fancy that after humbly working all day in the bath-rooms for the healing of bodies and for the salvation of the living, the Virgin is now working during the night for the healing of souls and for the salvation of the dead.

She it was who was turning the wheel of fire and spinning the flax of prayers of flame to weave garments for those souls who are only waiting for their paradisal vesture to escape from Purgatory!

Might I not as well go to bed? The mountain wind that blows at nightfall, though this afternoon was torrid, chills me to the bone; these jumps of temperature occur almost every day, and they are very trying; moreover, I am done up with running through the streets on various errands, always uphill or down. I go on my way, but how many will remain awake and stay up, for now there are neither days nor nights at Lourdes; the town is feverish and cannot sleep; the Esplanade, the terraces, the broad walk along the Gave, are still lighted up with electricity and will remain thus until dawn; the Grotto, behind its closed iron railings, will go on consuming its ever-increasing pile of candles.

Many pilgrims, sitting on the benches, will tell their beads before the statue, shining clear in the light of the wax-candles, till dawn comes; others will walk up and down, singing *Aves* to keep out the cold; others will lie clown at full length in the warmth in the church of the Rosary with its ever-open doors, and there they will slumber in their exhaustion, listening dreamily to the silver tinklings of the bells of the altar-servers; and lastly, others will go to the shelter in which pilgrims, tired to death, are heaped together helter-skelter; but by this time all the places have already been taken.

The awakening of these poor shelterers, whom I once took by surprise early in the morning, was frightful; and the sleep that lays them by the heels tonight is no better. There is the snoring of those who are ruined with having to digest heavy pork—butchers' stuff and bad wines; there are the sighs of those suffering from nightmare, and of dreaming women. Little fellows are sleeping between their mother's legs, using her stomach for a pillow, and there are stifled wailings when, tired of lying uncomfortably on her back, she turns over and upsets her child. The shelter is a sort of morgue in which the corpses lie fully dressed, but with their feet bare and steaming!

Then there is the grunting of the sleepers awakened by the icy draught from the opening of the door; this is the reverse of the medal seen by day, it is the return of the beast in the ruin wrought by a nap!

But this covered lodging is a matter of indifference to the true lovers of the Virgin who ramble up and down, absent-mindedly, in front of the Grotto. The majority of these have but little liking for the hubbub of the mob, and they take advantage of the calmness of these few hours to keep their chilly watch close to her, invoking her in peace.

Lourdes is a city of nightwalkers who make compensation, by their excessive overtime devotion, for the sinful excesses of the nightwalkers of other towns. It is right to acknowledge that, if the devil swoops down upon this place of pilgrimage, as upon all sanctuaries devoted to the Virgin, the defence put up by the faithful here is desperate, and for one deliberate fall that may occur after dark, there are hundreds of conversions obtained by these lonesome prayers, by these solitary upward flights of aspiration, during the lagging hours when the Madonna fails to get any more.

These prayers unite with the splendid sheaves of prayer brought by the Poor Clares, who begin their Office just now, at the very moment when all other communities have stopped.

And they participate in the power of the graces drawn down by the nuns of St Clare. What an admirable thing is this communion of souls who love and help one another, though they are unknown to one another!

In the forlorn hospital in which the sick, kept awake by the noise of the shouts and the chants which they hear outside, despair amidst their sufferings of being able to go to sleep, may not these united prayers perchance be the balm to relieve their torments during the rest of the night, while they are hoping that the Virgin, moved by so many efforts, may deign tomorrow, just when they expect it least, to work their cure?

XI

NOTHING happens as you think in this place; you live in the unforeseen. This morning I have again been to the hospital; the sick in whom I was interested are no longer there; they have left Lourdes by the night trains. The little White nun has recovered the use of her legs; after a few baths the swelling of her knee disappeared, and the knee joint is well and quite lissom; she went away cheerfully, walking without assistance. So I hope she will get back to her cloister thoroughly cured;[1] but the brat with his wooden gutter!

It appears that he has relapsed into a worse state than ever, and he was replaced, in his splint, in the railway-carriage in an almost dying condition!

This passes my comprehension altogether. The miracle that took place does not surprise me; but the miracle given with one hand and taken away with the

---

1 *Author's Note:* This was written two years ago (1904). Sister Justinian returned to Lourdes on a pilgrimage of thanksgiving. She was examined afresh, and there was no trace of the tuberculous coxalgia from which she suffered. Hence one may affirm that, having regard to the conditions in which it took place, her cure was really miraculous.

other, well, that completely floors me; I don't know where I am.

I know, indeed, that a miracle that does not last and does not stand the test of time is nothing of the kind; and yet, how is an extranatural intervention to be denied in the case of this child? A twisted leg is restored, a ring of abscesses dries up, a new skin forms beneath scabs ready to break away, health returns without any transition or convalescence, and so vigorously that the child can run about without flagging—and all this is instantaneous, like a flash of lightning, after a simple dip in a bath of dirty water; can it be explained on purely psychological grounds? I don't think so.

If, indeed, I fall back upon the arguments used by doctors who are determined to see nothing in the happenings at Lourdes but phenomena of suggestion and religious exaltation which are, according to them, the supreme panacea for most diseases, I arrive at conclusions that are manifestly absurd.

That people suffering from nervous maladies, that hysterical women may be cured by great excitement, is possible; as a matter of fact, I see a certain number of women at Lourdes to whom such theories are applicable; only, here, no one regards them as miraculously cured, no one pays much attention to them; but this is not a case of some important personage who may have auto-suggested himself by becoming convinced beforehand that he will be healed; we have to do with an urchin seven or eight years old; and you have only to see children bathed in the piscina to appreciate their state of mind at such a moment. They think no more of invoking the Virgin nor of being cured. They struggle and cry and shout in the hands of the infirmarians who are holding them; and, once in the water, they scream until they are taken out!

What sort of suggestion will you find, in such conditions as these, in the case of a child whose piety, moreover, often amounts to just nothing at all?

But if the case of the little boy from Belley, from a human point of view, is still unintelligible to me, I must confess that, from the divine point of view, it seems to me even more incomprehensible.

A man or woman who has reached the cachectic condition of the last stage of galloping consumption is brought, dying, to Lourdes, and is cured, perhaps in the piscina, perhaps during the procession of the Blessed Sacrament, perhaps apart from all that, may be alone or in a quiet corner; the cure takes place, not slowly and progressively, but in an instant. Several doctors examine the case and find no trace of any lesion; the patient walks, eats, drinks and sleeps just like you or me; a sort of resurrection has taken place; he goes away, and, sometimes, six months later, in his own home everything returns.

Clearly this is strange—for suggestion, after all, has never, so far as I know, brought anyone's lungs back again, even for six months, when they have once been "spewed out" (to use a vulgar expression); but we may, however, grant that when such people have been restored to their own homes, they returned to a life that defied all the laws of hygiene in the contaminated surroundings in which they contracted the disease that disappeared at Lourdes. A miracle is not, indeed, a vaccine which prevents those who have been cured by it from falling ill again, a serum that protects them even from the disease from which they were once cured; and, on the other hand, if you try to take the divine point of view, you may well suppose that the sick who have been restored to health may abuse the grace of God, and that their relapse may be a punishment; but such hypotheses as these will be in vain for such a case as that of the child from Belley. He had not changed his surroundings, nor could he, at his age, have misused the blessings he had received; the violent return of the malady cannot therefore be a sign of warning or of punishment; then, how can the irony of this sham miracle, the lie of its factitious validity, be explained? Is it a trap set by God's "ape," a repetition of the false visionaries whom he raised up in the days of the Virgin's apparitions to Bernadette, in order to create confusion and to cast a doubt upon the certainty of real miracles, or is it something else, and if so, what can it be?

I confess that this affair is the one that has stupefied me most at Lourdes, and the more closely I look into it the less I understand it, assuming, however, that the little urchin does not get well on his way back or when he is again in the hospital, for examples of such cures, accorded after a visit to the Virgin's domain and only when the place had been left behind, are abundant.

I tell myself, as I leave the hospital, that Lourdes is far from being as simple as Catholics and unbelievers think. To the former, everything is miraculous; to the latter, nothing is so; there is also something else, the most maddening mystery, as it strikes me, the thought of God either tolerating parodies or going back upon himself!

I go to the Convent of the Poor Clares in the same avenue, and on getting there I hand the portress a letter of introduction which I have received for her Abbess. I want to hear from her lips an account of a very special miracle that happened to her more than twenty years ago.

While waiting for an answer I take my place in the chapel. Its decoration is in perfect accordance with the expiatory lives of the nuns; it is a poor country shanty, extremely simple, with a meagre altar, furnished with wooden candlesticks, before the black trellis of the cloister; it is just right, it is just what it ought to be for an institution vowed to penance; it is almost deserted at this hour, and, sitting on a chair, I think upon this wonderful Order of St Clare, reformed by St Colette. Among the Orders of women it is certainly the one that has remained most faithful to its rule and the most intact; probably it is because of this constancy that it showed itself more resolute and brave than the rest under the tribulation; furthermore, one may say in honour of the children of St Francis, that they are the only ones who held fast to the last moment, the only ones today who have had the courage, while living at Paris, to wear their habit in the open street, like the Capuchins.

Anyhow, in Paris, instead of deserting like the Carmelites who left their outpost in the fight without a single blow, the Poor Clares have not left their prison-house in the Impasse de Saxe. Deprived of gardens and debarred from the open-air, they die there like flies, but gladly, making reparation for sins they know nothing of; they are now the only lightning-conductors of the city. And here at Lourdes, it is they again who endured the first assaults of the devil and put to their own account the misdeeds that have been done. Moreover, they are sometimes crushed down beneath incredible diseases that are not cured by the water of the Grotto.

Last year they were telling me of one of these holy women who was afflicted with such a swollen condition that she was more like a balloon than a woman; she could neither remain seated nor standing, and lying on her back was intolerable; it was not a case of dropsy; no one ever knew what it was; and she died with her face radiant, envied by her companions, and had to have a coffin specially made for her to be buried in.

How sad is this little Lourdes Convent dumped down along the edge of the torrent, the constant uproar of which it hears day and night! It is surrounded with a tiny sloping garden, and over the wall you can see the wooden crosses of its graveyard. The nuns have very little room for their walks; their life is dreadful and divine: continual fasts, never any meat, sleep cut in twain, the chapters of faults, and bare feet both winter and summer; and what do they live on? A few alms dropped into a sort of covered cooking-pan placed in the chapel; when this receptacle is empty, they ask for their food at the Bishop's; but they only get just enough to secure one meal for the day, for they are not allowed to have anything in hand, whether it be money or provisions; they must be poor, and these nuns are indeed poor for good!

This is rather unlike some of the other Orders, keen for gain and haunted with a mania for buildings which Providence has allowed to be swept off in the same way as the parings of piety from our land!

The Sister interrupts such reflections by coming to fetch me. She says that the Abbess is in the parlour, and, on leaving the chapel, she introduces me into a little white bare room, in which I take a seat in a rush-bottomed chair close to the iron grille furnished with spikes and further shut off behind its iron bars by a cast-iron plate with holes in it, like a skimmer; but instead of being round, they are elongated like the slits in a money-box, and our conversation, which is carried on with difficulty behind this iron sheeting which deadens our voices, begins. I ask the Abbess to give me a detailed account of the miracle I have been told about, and I hear the cheerful chuckle of an old woman accompanied by the more youthful laugh of the discreet Sister who is with her.

"Oh! that happened such a long time ago, Sir. Why, it is twenty-five years; only think of it!"

At last, without any further persuasion, she tells me her story:

She was a Sister, called Marie des Anges, in the house of the Poor Clares of St Colette in the Rue Sala, at Lyons, when, in 1867, after having taken her vows at the age of twenty-five, she was attacked by a cancerous affection of the right lobe of the liver. She was ill for three years, employed in the infirmary; then she had to take to her bed, and she remained bedridden for seven years; she could not feed herself and was so wasted away that her death was expected from day to day. Then it was that Mère Térèse, who had been sent two years previously to Lourdes with some of the Lyons nuns to found the present convent, wrote to the mother-house of the Rue Sala asking to be given Sister Marie des Anges.

"One of two things will happen," said she; "either she will get well, and that will show that our foundation of this convent is approved of by the Virgin; or else she will not recover, and then she will found the infirmary as our first sick case, and she will bring us a blessing as a suffering member of Christ."

"Our Mother of Lyons," added the Abbess after a moment's silence, "did not know what decision to take. She thought—and so did all the doctors—that I was too ill to undergo the fatigue of a journey to Lourdes. She asked what I thought, but I had no opinion on the subject; I was bound by my vow of obedience, ready to stay or go wherever they wanted me. Our Mother was still hesitating when the Archbishop of Lyons made a visit to the Abbey. Our Mother submitted the case to him in my presence. His Eminence thought that I ought to go, but when I asked him as my superior whether I should implore the Blessed Virgin to cure me, he replied thus, word for word: 'My daughter, I have no inspiration on the matter.'

"So I was put into the train and became the first sick case in the new convent. The journey was most distressing, but everyone was most attentive and kind to me all the way! They had to put me in a litter to get me out of the trains, and every time they moved me, I suffered the tortures of the cross. At last I got to the end of my journey, almost dead; they dragged me along as well as they could to the door of this convent, and Mother Teresa ordered me not to bathe and to ask for a cure.

"Thus I was taken to the Grotto—it was September 17, 1878—and there they lay me on the ground behind an altar on wheels, and left me.

"I could not tell whom I ought to obey, the Cardinal or the Abbess. Really I was distressed at the thought of recovering. Why, everyone said I had but a few days to live before I should be with God. At last, I was giving myself up to his will and weeping, when a bishop, followed by a gentleman of Lyons whom I knew, found his way into the Grotto. This gentleman pointed me out to the bishop, who asked me some questions. I explained to him how I came to be there, as well as I could, and I could scarcely speak for weakness. Then, thinking this prelate was my new superior, the Bishop of Tarbes, I said: 'My Lord, you are my master now, and I have to obey you: will you order me to get well?'

"He was taken by surprise and answered: 'My child, it is my will, if it be the Virgin's will.'

"I scarcely had time to formulate a prayer; a great shudder went through me, and I was projected into a standing posture. Mgr. Fonteneau—as I came to know afterwards—was not the Bishop of Tarbes but the Bishop of Agen, and he was my questioner. He was very pleased and gave me his blessing. Pilgrims ran up from every side and wanted to carry me off to the

Medical Records Office, but Père Sempé, who was then the Superior of the Missionaries of the Grotto and had been immediately informed of the miracle, was against it. 'She is outside her enclosure,' he said, 'let her go back to it as quickly as possible!'

"And that is all I have to tell you. Twenty-five years have passed away since then, and I have never been ill from that time."

"Why then, Reverend Mother, you did not at all want to get well?"

"No, indeed!" exclaimed Mother Marie des Anges with vivacity. "God be praised! but just think that I only live now to incur the responsibility of the office of an Abbess which I was not looking for, and that then I was ready—as far as one can be—to appear before the Lord!" And then she changed the conversation with a sigh, and told me how the good Mgr. Fonteneau never went to Lourdes as long as he was alive without coming to see her.

"And did you never return to the Grotto, even to make an act of thanksgiving?"

"No, for I cannot leave the enclosure. They tell me that the Grotto is much changed, and that iron railings have been put there owing to the crowds. In my own mind I always see it looking very simple, with just nothing at all, exactly as it was then."

I ruminate over this story after leaving the Abbess. Once more I think of the suggestion theory which is called upon to explain all the cures of Lourdes; but here is a nun who had no desire to recover her health and was cured in a manner in spite of herself! Had she made any use of autosuggestion, the result would have been exactly the opposite of what actually occurred; she would have died as she wished!

This theory is really too fine-drawn; it is quite threadbare! Never has therapeutic suggestion been known to cure, as happens at Lourdes, diseases of the lungs and liver, cancer and lupus; nor has it been found to give sight to the blind and hearing to the deaf. In truth, those who advocate this sort of treatment are obliged to admit, unless they are charlatans, that its results are most unreliable and most restricted. Unfortunately they barely succeed in quieting affections of the nerves, and this success they have been perpetually dinning into our ears for years past! If science is going bankrupt, it is owing to psychotherapy, just born and on the point of dying, that it is beginning to do so.

But on the other hand, what a splendid proof of the potency of the monastic vows has the Virgin given! For this miracle is a miracle of obedience; and I think of the little White Sister of the Holy Ghost from Brittany; who can tell whether she was not cured for the same reason? Was she so anxious to live? I remember her exclamation: "How glad our Mother will be!" She, too, came here by obedience and asked for recovery at her Superior's request, and she seemed better pleased for her Superior's sake than for her own when she was cured! Who can fathom the delightful depths of a soul so loosened from self and so lost in God?

Monastic obedience is so disorderly beneath its external regularity, so deep below its appearance of banal tranquillity, that it cannot be practised without a special helper from on High. A Superior, whether male or female, in other words, usually some fallible or mediocre individual, occupies in a monastery the place of Christ, and one has to become convinced that what they command is Christ's command, and that what they forbid Christ forbids. And then it is nothing to yield an outward obedience in all things, great or small, easy or hard, at all times and in all places, but obedience must be practised inwardly, with all the service of the mind and with perfect submission of heart!

Hence you will find it expedient to shut your eyes, and not to desire to inquire whether the order given is reasonable; subjection must be simple and trustful, without any mental reservation; it must be consentient and simple, facile and joyful!

This ideal is so contrary to human nature that there is no need to say that it is scarcely to be found in convents. Try to persuade yourself that you are going to give up without reservation and of your own entire accord all that constitutes your personality, all that differentiates you from your fellow men; bear in mind also that it will befit you to keep under the more or less conscious selfishness which is ever ready to urge you to take more interest in yourself than in your neighbour; fancy, furthermore, that you will have to give up all idea of seeking your own counsel and to be indifferent to humiliations and sufferings, that you will be merely a living tool in the hands of an Abbot whose character may be tyrannous or doddering, and that, when he presses the button, you will be virtually nothing but a machine turning upon its own inner mechanism in order to grind it to pieces—and you will imagine the volcano of rebellion which boils and growls within you, ready for an eruption!

And nevertheless there are human beings who love God so well and are so much beloved by him that they patiently and gladly submit to such a crushing of their wills, compelling themselves to hold their peace and submerging self in the happy indifference prepared for them by the divine pity. And such a one, methinks, is the good Abbess of the Poor Clares; but for one who exactly corresponds with her divine vocation to the cloister, how many others have I known—people of real goodness though they were—who, after having gone into the convents in which it appeared to be the will of God that they should be, when they could stand no more, have left them.

These, after having endured many humiliations without too much kicking against the pricks, rebelled all of a sudden against orders that seemed to them uncalled-for and doubtless were so. Here was their trial; they deliberated and were lost; in a moment the little which they had gained by abnegation crumbled to pieces; they ought to have cast everything away and to have kept nothing of self, they should have forsaken themselves entirely and annihilated themselves. They knew it, but nature overcame grace; and such, with rare exceptions, is now the case of all.

An admirable monk who had risen to be the Father General of one of the great Orders once said to me: "Brother so-and-so whom you knew is dead; well, you won't find his equal in any cloister now." And when I objected and said I had seen most pious lay brothers and ardent novices in one of his novitiate communities, he replied: "Yes, no doubt, you will still find saintly souls, but no more saints"; and he added: "You give them an order, and they carry it out at once; but they ransack their minds to discover why the order was given them, and hence they are inevitably led on to the discussion of its claims. That is enough to weaken the virtue of obedience; it ceases to be generous, spontaneous and complete; God's blessing is forfeited as soon as it begins to argue."

What is the reason of it? In the case of men, it is chiefly due to compulsory military service, for although it may help seminarians by teaching them a knowledge of life, it is yet deplorable for novices in religion who need no instruction in barrack-room talks and in matters which they will perhaps find it very hard to forget in their cells.

In any case, when they are in military training they learn a sort of grousing discipline, an obedience submitted to but detested; they learn to be on the watch and to be suspicious, to dispute the honesty of some of the instructions, and they carry away with them into their monasteries the leaven, if not of rebellion, at any rate of discussion.

In a still more general way, this also comes from the morbid condition of society now too much deceived by lying ostentation and the abuse of outward show. The scandals of the day which were doubtless formerly unrevealed but are now spread by the press into the remotest corners of the country, have long since relieved us of the sense of respect, deprived us of deferential regard.

No one now believes in the honesty of politicians, in the gallantry of generals, in the independence of magistrates; no one imagines that the clergy consist of saints. Refusing to acknowledge the exceptions that are really to be found, they have flung képis, mortar-boards and birettas into the same bag to be shot on to the rubbish-heap; indeed, there is now a kind of malaria of disrespect, and no one escapes this spiritual infection; everyone has caught it to some extent, for we cannot avoid the atmosphere in which we live and still less the diabolical influences that make themselves now more strongly felt than ever before, for the devil is in all that we think or say; it is like the very air that we breathe.

How far are we now from monastic obedience which, I fear, will become disintegrated in this increasingly corrosive environment! Happy indeed, how happy is such a genuine nun as Mère Marie des Anges, who never sees and who will never know anything of all this!

Well, instead of spinning such tiresome reflections I should do far better by going to confession, but unfortunately that is no easy matter. The Crypt beneath the Basilica, in which are installed the confessionals of the clergy who have taken the place of the Fathers belonging to the Grotto, is inaccessible since the influx of the international pilgrimages. Furthermore, you might really suppose that the usual stupidity of the architects has here broken forth more violently than anywhere else. Last year, when you came to the Crypt you found a circular passage as soon as you entered, and it led you to the sacristy of the priest on duty; pilgrims had to find another way to get into the chapel and did not block your path; thus everyone had what he wanted. This year, all is altered; the circular passage has been done away with and there is only one way of getting into the Crypt, so that the hustling of people coming and going takes place in the poor tunnel in which everyone is crushed to death. As for reaching the sacristy, that is quite an adventure, for you must allow yourself to be jostled hither and thither by the flux and reflux of strangers in the single passage, and then, all at once, get free and cut through another crowd of people filling up the cellar, in order to reach the box assigned to the confessor.

This Crypt, when it is not temporarily inaccessible, is the least offensive of the churches of Lourdes. Little, short, very low, bristling with pillars, and badly illuminated with electric bulbs alight all day, it nevertheless has a touch of privacy about it, a little shelter far from the noisy flow of the crowd. When the mobs do not conglomerate here, you can find solitude in the shadow of a pillar; and then its ornamentation is more intelligent and less vulgar than that of the other churches. Above each of its altars, which are set in half-moon-shaped recesses, it has deep embrasured windows cut slantingly into the thickness of the walls, and the embrasures are covered with gold mosaics. And here one can better than anywhere else take account of the part this kind of ornamentation should play in monumental art, for here it is set free from its bootless desire to imitate pictures as it does in the chapels of the Rosary, and from straying off into portraiture as in the two ridiculous pastilles stuck over the doorway of the Rosary and pretending to reproduce the features of Pope Leo XIII and Mgr. Schoepfer, the Bishop of Tarbes.

Here the mosaics are satisfied with interlacing arabesques, foliage, flowers and crosses worked in coloured stones on a background of crackled gold; and, in the dim daylight from the loopholes and in the orange beams of the electric almonds, the embrasures glitter with the fawn-tinted smoky gleaming of old gold seen on Cordova leather; and these sinuous and dull glimmerings make a most sumptuous and discreet decoration of this markedly white vault. In this Crypt better than anywhere else you can see early in the morning at Mass the contrast that is clearly evident between the lights of the electric pouches and that of the wax-candles burning on the altar. Nothing is less symbolical than this style of illumination which has been adopted not only at Lourdes but in Paris in most churches, and even in some abbey chapels. It is, indeed, a real contradiction to make use of inanimate lights where Christ dwells whose living image is light; it also means that the Church is doing away with the indispensable Sign of Charity, of which fire is the emblem; and here we are far away from the divine liturgy with its venerable and magnificent form of blessing for the oil and the wax, with our bundles of incandescent wires, the least disadvantage of which is that it makes false light, for it does not illuminate, and it is impossible to read the Office by it in the sallow beams which let their golden light be diluted and diffused as it descends from the arches overhead.

What has become of the queer specimens who used to frequent the Crypt during the calmer periods of our Lourdes? Of Mary the cripple, who used to bounce up the terrace of the Rosary in her wooden dish which the Fathers of the Grotto used to renew when it was worn out? Of the bedridden woman sitting in a wheeled chair, which was wheeled in and out at the entrance to the Crypt at the end of the aisle leading to the high altar? Thus she used to attend the ten o'clock Mass, and the priest went right down the church to give her Holy Communion; then she was fetched away in her perambulating dwelling at midday.

You could never make out her face; it was covered with such thick veils that I used to wonder—before I came to know that she had been afflicted for twenty-five years with a disease of the spine—whether she was hiding a putrefying head beneath the face-band which she pulled up just above her nose to receive the Host—and then she would lower it again immediately afterwards.

And those two dreadful creatures, two immensely wealthy sisters, who had made a vow five years previously on the feast of St Benedict Labre, to live as he did in a winding-sheet of filth; both wore rags beneath their dresses and spared themselves the trouble of ever undressing or washing; the elder one, with wild eyes and features blackened in with the dust that filled her wrinkles, had her chignon full of warrens of fleas which ran along her shoulders to meet another colony of insects nesting in her bodice. The younger one was no cleaner but kept herself free from the vermin that devoured her sister by having her hair, beneath her crepe veil, shorn close.

They stank like the stalls of a knacker's yard, and people fled at their approach.

Also what has become of the hare-brained pietists and maniacs who used to go up and down the terraces, entering the vestibule of the Crypt and making one genuflection here and another there? Down below at the Grotto they kissed the ground, got up went to drink at the spring, returned to kiss the ground, went on to kiss the rock and drank again; and all this hour after hour!

This year they have been lost in the immense crowds of pilgrims, and I have not seen them once.

To return to the Crypt; today I have to take my place in the queue of pilgrims to get in; the air is unbreathable; I make some progress behind people's backs in a reek of miasmas; at last, after pushing and being pushed I get free from those packed around me, and passing across the benches which are loaded with the faithful whom I disturb, I reach the sacristy; it is full! This is discouraging; I say to myself: I will go to confession another day, but another day it will be just the same so long as the railway companies continue to discharge their train-loads of passengers in the Lourdes valley.

If the penitents were all men, the laundry-work would be soon over, for the laundrymen usually have quickly done with the men after a summary cleansing; but the women! They, indeed, not only want to be starched, but ironed afterwards; and then, if only each of them brings all her little family affairs to the wash and the laundryman takes some interest in them, it will go on for hours!

However, I make up my mind to stay on. As there are no chairs I stand in a corner and survey my neighbours. The firstcomers are men; there they are with bowed heads peeling their consciences; they will soon have done dumping their bundles of parings at the priest's feet, and I take comfort in observing that most of the women are of the peasant class; they will be less lengthy in recounting their exploits and also sooner dismissed than the middle-class ladies.

Perhaps I shall not be kept waiting too long; but nevertheless how ill-managed now is the hearing of confessions, which was so well organised by the Fathers of the Grotto when they were the masters of Lourdes! Here are but a few ecclesiastics who are unequal to the task, and unfortunately all these churchmen brought along by the pilgrimages, and given on demand the power of hearing confessions, do not seem to be at all anxious to come to the assistance of their brethren; they regard themselves as boys on a holiday and are not at all eager—unless it be to dust the inner chambers of a few of their Philotheas—to intern themselves in the stuffy confessional-boxes. Some, indeed, especially the younger ones, take their place among the bands of infirmarians, but they would do much better to leave this material work to laymen in order to devote their attention to the service of souls who also want to have their wounds dressed.

There are two of them just now on duty. Splendid fellows! they don't dilly-dally. You hear the constant rattle of the sliding shutters; men with reddened faces slip out, casting aside the curtain behind which they were in shelter, and are off at top speed, like cats flying over hot bricks; but the women show no such shame-facedness; they are quite at home in the confessional and take pleasure in it, and withdraw but slowly and with regret to make room for others who come to scent the aroma of sins which still floats about the box, and to add thereto the more or less marked perfume of their own.

But not one of them is the least put out by being seen. A man's desire is to get it all over and be off; the woman's is to spin things out and to stay on.

I pity the poor priest who swings like a pendulum from one side to the other in his cupboard provided with a shutter, and drilled with holes like a sieve. How hot he must be! Though I am not interned as he is, I am suffocating in this air, saturated as it is with spiritual dregs and effluvia of perspiring passers-by. I would give a great deal to get away; at last it is my turn; I empty my basket into the ears of an excellent man who gives me absolution in a trice, and then fly from the sacristy; but now the question is, how to pack off from the Crypt; the two streams of the crowd keep on flowing in opposite directions through the narrow aisle, and I have to make sturdy use of my elbows to get out.

Here I am at last! It is extraordinary what relief confession gives, and how light and fit you feel afterwards; your sense of it is almost physical. Really there is a virtue, which is perceptible and almost tangible, in the sacrament of Penance!

XII

OLD Lourdes is destitute of display; it is a little
provincial town adorned with a town hall, a law
court, and a great square graced with a fountain. As soon
as it rains you slither about, churning up the swampy
mud into a sort of thick broth; directly the sun shines,
you are fried. When the pilgrimage season is over, you
have the peace of an old country town, broken only
by the hubbub of fair-days; then the square becomes
a swaying harvest of blue caps and black hoods; the
peasants of the neighbourhood bring to market little
bullocks with the horns of bisons, little cows that have
never been milked with great hard udders, sheep scattering their liquorice drops all over the ground as they
jostle one another, white pigs with black spots, looking as if they had been stuffed with truffles while still
alive, goats and poor little kids, flung on the ground
with their four legs tied together as if they were dead;
and all around this menagerie are stretched long rows
of flat baskets, open to the breeze, in which Spanish
rose-tinted onions spotted with dull wine-stains are
offered for sale, and strings of garlic, round cheeses of

the texture of putty beneath their dirty crust of rind, butcher's meat, esparto-soled shoes, hairy fabrics, old iron, lemons and hideous earthen ware pots with chocolate-coloured bellies, striped with streaks of buttery yellow; there is something of all sorts, devotional odds and ends at a penny a bundle and loaves of white bread, a treat for the mountaineers who usually eat nothing but black bread.

And amidst the lowing of the cows, the bleating of the sheep, the grunting of the pigs, all these people are jabbering stick in hand, sitting at the tables outside the cafés and calling out to one another; the old men, with hard faces and hooked noses joined on to their mouths by furrows like sword slashes; the young men, with faces of roystering privates. With but few exceptions all the old men are clean-shaven and all the young fellows have moustaches; and all are in caps and wearing hunting jackets and hooded cloaks; all are shod, especially the old men, with incredible sabots, the front of which turns upwards like the prow of a galley with the curved blade of a yataghan.

The race appears to have retained something of its ancient savagery; you feel that it is still brutal and proud, rough in dealing with animals, almost cruel in a latent fashion, and only civilised by having to buy and sell; you feel that it is full of tenacity and courage, but also pugnacious; and it is quite certain that if, during the Combes ministry, and as some of the male termagants of the Bloc demanded, they had forbidden pilgrimages and closed the Grotto, all these wild-boar hunters would have shouldered their guns and fought in the mountains. The Virgin would have had the advantage of their obstinate defence of their own interests, but our French Iscariot knew it and lay low.

It is not market-day today in old Lourdes, but it is none the less crammed with people, for the streets are blocked with pilgrims standing outside the shops of devotional articles on which the name of Soubirous may be read and notices proclaim that the proprietor is a brother or relative of Bernadette; for the family waves her name as a sort of trade flag. Like all houses that have become historic from a religious point of view, this one is decorated with a few portraits of the heroine and pious pictures of various degrees of ugliness. It is a miserable hovel furnished with a few household utensils and with Bernadette's bed enclosed with a railing to protect it from the fanatics who had already begun to cut off chips with their knives to make the bits of wood into relics.

And here, that is all that is left of the holy girl whose revelations have transformed this hitherto unknown hole into a town celebrated throughout the world.

This dark and dirty and scarcely swept room gives you the impression of being a forsaken tomb, without a wreath or a flower, in a disused cemetery; and you begin vituperating the forgetful selfishness of Lourdes which has renewed its youth since the apparitions of the Virgin to her child, especially since, thanks to her, people are flocking thither in multitudes. It has been transformed, to tell the truth more plainly, from a village into a town. Luxurious shop-windows, various kinds of groceries, first-class confectioners, have now replaced on the ground floors along the streets the poor dwellings in which the passer-by used to see old women in spectacles sitting at work in the window-frames. The countrymen are now hotel-keepers and sellers of wax-candles, and their wives have changed into fine ladies who parade in startling dress on Sundays. They live at their ease and without the least trouble they might realise ample fortunes if the rage for display and the certainty that the fleecing of pilgrims will go on forever did not spur them on into spending even more than they get.

If the Virgin were to abandon the Grotto tomorrow, all these people who have erected sumptuous hotels would succumb beneath the burden of debt, and it would mean the selling up of all the dealers in the devotional line, and the general bankruptcy of Lourdes.

As for their religion, if you would gauge its true value, it would have to stop bringing in profits. It may all be summed up in the remark of one who lived among them and knew them well: "Human respect is turned upside down in this place." In Paris, for fear of being pointed out, men hide in order to do their Easter duties; at Lourdes, you find just the opposite; men do them openly to escape being noticed, and of course never go to church again afterwards. I fear that such religion may be only part of the window-dressing of the devotional bazaars; it helps, in any case, to hook purchasers; it contributes towards the increase of cash sales.

Formerly, on entering the town I used to go to old St Peter's, which was a charming country church. Picture to yourself a romanesque building, indifferently repaired, but still preserving to some extent the character of the thirteenth century; it possessed old coloured woodwork, and amongst this was a statue of Our Lady of Mount Carmel offering a scapular to St Simon Stock, and above all a little statue of the Virgin sauntering along with a touch of affectation and smiling with astonished eyes in an ecstatic face. For once at Lourdes you found yourself looking at a Madonna who was not new and walls which were not white!

Very silent, hardly lighted at all, and very intimate, it was almost empty on week-days, and when you had freed yourself from the crowds in new Lourdes, what a delightful refuge it provided! The few women who were praying before the Blessed Sacrament remained motionless in their chairs and dumb; there was not a sound. How different was this deep piety, sure enough of itself to be calm, from the agitation and frenzy of the pilgrims at the Basilica and the Rosary! It seemed as if Mary herself felt the effect of this soothing atmosphere, of these unhurried prayers, of these placid supplications. You received a vague impression that, instead of standing upright to await her visitors as she does in all the other churches of the town, here she remained seated, more at her ease, more in the family, and in deeper tranquillity. You could talk to Her sweetly and at length in the silence and the dimness.

And on Sunday the nave used to be full at the High Mass. The men were few, but there were many women and girls who, in their black dresses and hoods, instantly made you think of nuns at prayer in an old cloister chapel; and in this poor village church the divine service seemed almost luxurious. There were nice bands of choir-boys, in clean surplices and violet caps, a great beadle in red, a choir of little mountaineers and a few choir-men with metallic voices who sang plainchant.

I often used to take refuge there, happy in following the Mass in peace and in not having to listen to tol-de-rol-lols.

This church exists no longer. The Vandals have cast it down, and, to replace it, they have built, a little farther on, a sort of cathedral which is to the romanesque style what the Basilica is to the gothic—that is to say, a nauseating marvel of cheapness.

To demolish an old church, the floor of which was worn smooth by centuries of prayer, full of memories of Bernadette, in order to put in its place a clumsy monument trying to beat the Basilica with its frightful coloured windows and other false glitter, what an aberration! And it wins with ease, with its waggoner's architecture and heavy obtuse nave, at the head of which rises a high altar of variegated marbles, like an assortment of Italian cheeses and galantine and forcemeat, entirely covered with an enormous ciborium of cardboard and wood frosted over with gilding. It is like the scenery of a Punch and-Judy show. What a barbarian was he who invented such reprisals as these! And to crown his work he found it necessary to add a little more gilding to the dazzling ensemble of his other tinsel finery, and no doubt after much reflection he resolved to stretch gilded chains across the side-chapels. What can you think of such a fellow?

Was this wonderful temple erected for the worship of a Marquis de Carabas or for the worship of God?

As for the old wooden statues, there is no need to say that they have disappeared, and the bad quarters of Saint-Sulpice now contaminate all the altars with their villainous products.

Ah! this new church which was built only to score off the Basilica, to set altar against altar, to use the words of Cardinal Langénieux, how it evokes, just taken by itself, all the episodes in the history of Lourdes, the subterranean battles fought between the two parties of the rector Peyramale and old Lourdes, secretly manoeuvred by M. Lasserre, and that of the Bishops of Tarbes and the Fathers of Garaison.

Though I do not want to stir the cinders which are still smouldering between the two parties, I am going to explain how Mgr. Peyramale, who was the rector of Lourdes at the time of the Apparitions, killed his old church with a light heart, for pecuniary reasons and for the good of his parish, and also out of vexation when he saw the district of the Grotto separated from his cure.

Mgr. Peyramale was an excellent man and a very good priest, but he was a rude countryman, obstinate and crabbed by nature, and furthermore, a sort of megalomaniac and muddler. But a good businessman with a clear head and a more supple temperament than his was needed to set on foot the gigantic undertaking of Lourdes. With him nothing would have gone right. His bishop, Mgr. Laurence, saw this, and he betook himself to Père Sempé, who possessed the qualities of skilfulness and prudence which he considered indispensable to the success of the work. He therefore restricted Peyramale to his own parish and put Père Sempé at the head of the Garaison missionaries whom he summoned to Lourdes to organise the service of Masses and confessions and sermons, and to direct the processions and put up the pilgrims, whose numbers were constantly increasing in a town which was then no more than a small village, a fearful hole.

With the best will in the world Peyramale with his three assistant clergy could not have undertaken such a task, and it is extremely probable that if the missionaries, instead of being under the rule of Pete Sempé, had been placed beneath his rod, he would never have thought of making any complaints, for he could not deny the necessity of some such reinforcements; but, vexed at being set aside, hurt at having been rather brutally, it must be admitted, dispossessed, while he was ill, of the Basilica which he had built above the Grotto; finding poor consolation in the dignity of Monsignor, which his bishop managed to get raised to a Roman prelacy, he resolved—although this had never been asked for by the Virgin—to erect another basilica in the town itself.

A pretext had to be found. His first argument was the insufficiency of his church, which he thought too ugly to compete with that of the Grotto; then he conceived the absurd fancy that the Virgin's message to Bernadette meant this: that the pilgrimages, instead of going straight from the railway-station to the spring, ought to start from the village church, from his own church, marching in procession to the Basilica, and thence come back again to his church.

194

And in his paper, the *Echo des Pélerins*, his friend and counsellor Lasserre carried these mystificatory pleasantries still farther, maintaining that "it is not the Grotto but old Lourdes which ought to be the centre for the pilgrimages, that the Virgin is invoked by the name of 'Our Lady of Lourdes' and not as 'Our Lady of the Grotto,' and the village church ought to be the first and the last station for the pilgrimages."

As may well be supposed, this proposition was supported by old Lourdes, which wanted in this way to be able to fleece the pilgrims both on the way there and on the way back.

Moreover, the unfortunate rector, possessed as he was by a mania for bigness, launched forth without stint into the expense of raising vast buildings; he ran terribly into debt, and left behind such an encumbered estate when he died on September 8, 1877, that bishop after bishop in the see of Tarbes had to go through years and lawsuits, each one more deeply embroiled than the last, to get it liquidated.

These ineptitudes help us to form an opinion of how he would have administered the property of the Grotto, if the bishop had entrusted the management of it to him. From all the above it seems to me perfectly clear that the notion of building, far from the place of Apparitions, far from the spring, far from the Esplanade and the shelters, a basilica which could be of no interest or advantage to the pilgrims, must have been utterly absurd, unless its object was to extract money for the benefit of the caterers and rosary-sellers of old Lourdes, and, at the same time, to erect a rival memorial to be set against another memorial.

I may add that there could be no serious reason to justify the destruction of the charming old church, for it was quite large enough, whatever Peyramale may have said about it, to hold all his flock. I have myself proved this on Sundays; there was room enough in it for the whole of the village. If the rector wanted a chapel for teaching the catechism, it was an easy matter to build one quite cheaply on the very spot where the new basilica makes such a parade. Lastly, if it was in a very dilapidated condition, it ought to have been repaired and made secure; this was quite practicable with a good architect.

When we think that these barbarous exploits were due to the rivalry between Peyramale and Sempé, we cannot help deploring the exclusiveness which was the common failing of both of these priests—and let us confess that it is a characteristic of almost all the Pyrenean clergy—that they cannot endure any neighbour's influence or co-operation in their activities.

What is also indisputable is that both Peyramale and Sempé displayed the aesthetic principles of the Fuegians and the ideals of the omophagi. In that they were agreed. To the one we owe the Basilica and the new church; to the other, the Rosary: the two make a pair, the one as good as the other.

Now to come to the present, I do not think that Zola's criticisms of the Fathers of the Grotto are justified in the book in which he has collected together all the complaints that Lasserre had already charged them with in his heap of articles and romances.

As the Abbé Moniquet very clearly shows, with evidence to prove it, in his two books *Le Cas de M. Lassere* and *Les Origines de Notre-Dame de Lourdes*, Lasserre did not succeed as he wished to do in "imposing his personality and book" on the Bishops of Tarbes and the Garaison Fathers, and this rebuff so stirred him to retaliate that we may well suspect the equity of his judgements and even the honesty of his stories.

But let us come to the charges made. Are the Lourdes missionaries wealthy and do they sell statues, water and wax-candles? Yes, it cannot be denied—and I don't congratulate them or their successors on it—but upon this question follows another: how do they spend the money thus acquired?

Now, it is quite clear that if their receipts are on a colossal scale, so are their expenses. You must remember that within the domain of the Grotto everything is gratis. In order to guard against simony as far as possible, Père Sempé would not allow priests to pay for their Masses as they are bound to do in other pilgrimages; and when you remember that such Masses run to hundreds of thousands a year; if you reckon up the cost of altar-linen, wine and Hosts for celebrants and communicants, who sometimes number one hundred and forty thousand communions a month; if you further take into account the lack of cleanliness and the carelessness of priests in transit who soil and tear decorations which often require renewal, you get amazing figures. It is also right to recollect that the chairs in the churches bring in nothing, that the baths in the piscinas are gratis; above all it is well to bear in mind the enormous expense of the upkeep of the churches and the choirs, of the Esplanade and the gardens, of the clinic and the refuges, the cost of servants, the Sisters who do the washing, the electric light burning night and day, the entertainment of bishops and of the directors of pilgrimages at the community house, the alms and all the rest; and if you made out a balance-sheet, you would no doubt find that the collections, the gifts and the offerings that flow in from all sides would not suffice to equal the outgoings, unless the sale of the water which is sent far away and that of the wax-candles used on the spot were to convert a certain loss into a profit.

In fine, the Fathers have only claimed a single monopoly, that of the water despatched in bottles or cases; otherwise, in Lourdes itself, everyone is allowed to draw and to carry away with him as much water as he pleases without paying a penny.

In any case, it is the poor who gain from such prosperity, and they would do ill to complain of it. Here, they are treated as they are nowhere else. They have nothing to pay, either in the church or in the refuges. Let us add that there are no reserved seats nor special prie-dieu in the Basilica or the Crypt or the Rosary; hence there is perfect equality between rich and poor. Show me another church where you will find the like!

As for the traders of old Lourdes, I take no more interest in them than in those of the new, and I do not understand why Zola was more smitten with one set than with the other. Most of them are cormorants who fight one another, if not for the skin, at any rate for the purses of the visitors.

Besides, do not the people of old Lourdes, suddenly improvised during the pilgrimages into hotel and restaurant keepers and dealers in rosaries and medals, make their profits easily enough? Do not they all sell statues and wax-candles as well as the Fathers? Have the latter kept the sale of these things to themselves?

It was not the Fathers, indeed, who invented the commercial degradation of making the Lourdes water bonbons and lozenges provided by the shop keepers! No; after all, I cannot get rid of the notion that the old grudge of Lourdes against its bishops and missionaries, "those monomaniacs of possession" as Lasserre calls them, is above all due to the fact that they bought up the landed estates which look down upon the Grotto from the opposite side of the Gave. If these could have been purchased by the people of the place, they would have fitted up sumptuous hotels there, with garages and grand suppers; some day or other the two banks would have been linked up by throwing a bridge across them; the army of English and American tourists from Pau, Bagnères, Argelès and Luchon would have held high festival on the terrace of a first-class hotel as they looked down upon the processions and invocations, and the benedictions with the Blessed Sacrament, and the miracles wrought at the spring. They would have occupied the front boxes and paid for the necessary extras; piles of money would have been made.

The Fathers, however, have left the fields in pasture, and purchased them just for the purpose of preventing such scandals as these! Had the bishop and Père Sempé achieved no more than that, they would nevertheless have merited highly of our Lady!

So Zola, who picked up his information in the most cursory manner, does not appear to have taken full account of the inner workings of the situation at Lourdes.

Had he any clearer insight when he tried to give us a full-length portrait of Bernadette—of whom, however, he speaks with affection, as he also spoke with respect of the Virgin, whom Catholic publications inexplicably accuse him of dragging through the mire? I think not, for he represents her as both a mystic and a victim of hysteria.

But never was anyone less of a mystic than Bernadette, nor was she a person deranged by hysteria.

How many doctors carefully watched her with regard to this question! And not one of them was able to discover the least trace of that sort of infirmity from the day of her birth till the day of her death. Hence they were driven, in order to explain the Apparitions, to assert that she was, if not mad—which was impossible, since it was easy to convince anyone that she was not—at any rate afflicted with some mental trouble, hallucinated.

But then, what a singular case of hallucination was this little girl who only suffered from it just long enough to reveal and to establish the Virgin's work, and never showed any signs of hallucination before or since! On the other hand, admitting the soundness of a theory which is in vogue with many alienists, hallucination is always a more or less impaired reminiscence of some sensation formerly experienced; it is not, therefore, a case of invention but of recollection.

How then could Bernadette have recalled words which she had never heard? How could she have discovered a spring she knew nothing of, the presence of which in the Grotto was as unsuspected by every one else as by herself? How could she have imagined a type of the Virgin which she had never seen in any print or picture, since it was unknown before her day, and has become a special ikon, a new figure in devotion, entirely owing to her? Lastly, how came she to put into the Virgin's mouth the expression "Immaculate Conception," of which she had never heard, nor did she even understand its meaning?

Then how are we to explain—if she was hallucinated—her coming to the Grotto several times, expecting the Virgin to be there when She never came? Hence the apparitions depended neither on her will power nor upon the strength of her belief.

She was of a lymphatic nature, nervous, puny and small; at thirteen she looked as if she were only twelve; her face was pleasing and her make delicate; she was suffering with asthma; such is a strictly correct description of her; there are many children of a like constitution who are no more hysterical nor unbalanced than she was.

The portrait drawn by such adversaries of the supernatural as Zola is, indeed, no true likeness; but are those depicted of her by such Catholic writers as Lasserre, who make of her an angel and a plaster saint fit for a niche, any better?

It seems to me that, if you want to find a fairly accurate representation of Bernadette, you must examine records which were not written from memory long afterwards, like those of Estrade which may be unintentionally imperfect, and also such documents as appeared before legend took possession of her.

Therefore I have run through the papers of her day, the *Annales de la Grotte* edited by the Garaison Fathers, who were in close touch with her and set down what they saw with great simplicity, so that you can trace in what they wrote no suspicion of anxiety to depreciate or to decorate her.

This is what may be found in Vol. II—Second Year—on April 30, 1869:

"Bernadette was good-natured, gentle, simple and naïve; she was edifying but not extraordinary. She was a child whose wit was rather lacking in versatility, and her imagination was somewhat dull; she could not be very talkative; it was not her charm of conversation that won over a whole people to believe in apparitions, and no one was more unfitted to arouse enthusiasm; she had no gift of description nor power to interest anyone; her narrative was curt, colourless and cold; you had to keep on questioning her to get a full description of what she had seen.

"She spoke without any sign of feeling; she became rather more lively after a time, but her joy was never of an ardent kind . . . she was, indeed, extremely commonplace.

"She appeared to be grave and attentive in her religious practices, but her devotion never rose to the level that many people expected of her after the unheard-of grace of having received eighteen visions."

Lastly, the Abbé Pomian, her confessor up to the time she went to Nevers, said of her:

"Nothing distinguished her from common children. She was left uneducated; she hardly had an ordinary amount of intelligence. . . ."

These are not flattering portraits, but that is only a further reason for thinking that they may be true.

First of all, note what the Fathers say of her lack of imagination; we may conclude from this that here we have but one more proof of the truth of her stories, for she must have been incapable of making them up—and also note the low level of her devotion.

"Her piety was sincere, but there was nothing of the enthusiast or of the *exalté* about it." So said the Superior General of the Sisters of Nevers after Bernadette had entered the community. Moreover, Bernadette herself proves the simplicity of her devotion. When asked to give a special form of prayer, she answered: "The rosary is my favourite form of prayer, I am too ignorant to make one up." And when one of the Superiors of her convent, becoming impatient of exercises that seemed to her too childish, exclaimed: "At your age, you ought to go into the chapel sometimes and meditate a little!" she replied gently: "Really, I don't know how to meditate."

Here we are far from the mysticism which is put before us. We can see that her fervour was of a restricted and somewhat routine order, and therefore incapable of having turned her head and induced the hallucinations which Zola talks about.

On the other hand, the rather slow intelligence and the dull and cramped understanding of the child afford a further corroboration of the experimental fact that God chooses only the poor and the lowly when he requires an interpreter to speak on his behalf to the multitude.

Indeed, it would have been difficult to find a more poverty-stricken family in Lourdes, and, it must be said, one of poorer repute than that of Bernadette, who was herself run down on account of her relations.

Père Cros, S.J., who consulted all the archives and examined the depositions of more than two hundred witnesses, tells us that the destitution of the Soubirous was so extreme that they often went without bread, and that one of Bernadette's little brothers used to scratch off the wax dropping from the candles on to the floor at Masses for the dead, to eat it.

At the end of March, 1857, when the family had reached the utmost point of destitution, the head of the Soubirous family—although innocent, I believe—was taken up and imprisoned at Lourdes until the following April 4, charged with stealing flour and wood.

Discredit ensued upon poverty. God willed that there should be abasement, and he had it.

Therefore he took this man's daughter, and he took her just as she was, humble and pure, gentle and good, but really "of no account," to use the very words of the Fathers. He wrought no miracle for her when he raised her at a stroke to himself. He made no difference between her and her companions, and left her a simple peasant, in every sense of the word; for this actual detail recorded by Père Cros, that as soon as she ceased to be in ecstasy and the Virgin had departed from her, she went on scratching the fleas beneath the handkerchief on her head as usual, is typical.

But does she not thus appear to be more human and true to life than she does in all the pictures in which she is transformed into a little fairy shepherdess? As a matter of fact, she was only squared off after she went into the cloister; for there she finished learning to read and write; her intelligence did not improve, even her piety did not rise to a higher level, but her charming gifts of gentleness and humility, which she already possessed, increased. She who in ecstasy had reflected in her transfigured look as in a far-off mirror the vision of our Lady's features, henceforward had but one desire, to hide the reflection and its recollection behind the veil; she yearned to be forgotten far from the crowds. She never showed any vanity or self-love, and God knows what adulation she received as "the good little virgin," for so the peasant-women called her! Ashamed of such worship, she used to say with a sigh: "What a queer creature I must be." Once, hearing some people behind her say: "If only I could cut off a bit of her dress!" she turned round and cried out, not in anger, but in a tone of firm conviction: "How silly you are!"

In the cloister, in order to keep her in the way of renunciation, she was often humiliated before those who honoured her most, and she never showed any sign of vexation nor uttered a single word of complaint.

She wanted to be a Carmelite, but her health was not strong enough for the severe régime of their unbending rule; so she went into the Convent of St Gildard, belonging to the Sisters of Charity of Nevers. There she proved a most charitable infirmarian and a most docile nun; her two and only infirmities of rustic obstinacy and sulkiness disappeared by degrees. God purified her, carrying through the task which she could not herself fulfil. "She was worked upon by him more than she could work upon herself," states Abbé Febver, the community chaplain. In any case, she was delightfully pure in soul when the Lord took her away from the cloister bouquet. She suffered greatly before dying. Her sufferings made her wither away; she became, in the words of the Mother General, "so thin that she almost appeared to have no flesh on her bones."

If the religious who tended her are to be believed, her body revived after her death and her face looked once more young and charming in its repose; during the last three days before her burial her limbs were flexible and her hands retained their natural colour and the ends of her fingers were rosy. Moreover, no humour nor smell nor other trace of dissolution was observable when she was laid to rest in a chapel dedicated to St Joseph and erected in the Convent garden.

The Virgin had kept her word. She had not made her "happy in this world," but She certainly kept her other promise, "to make her happy in the next."

Let it be added that if Free Thought has always refused to admit the revelations of Soubirous' daughter, the church of Tarbes was no less suspicious at the beginning, and Bernadette had to submit to every sort of vexation at the hands of the clergy of Lourdes.

First of all Père Sempé, as free from mysticism as any priest ever was, would not listen to her; the bishop, Père Cros informs us, who was a prudent and frigid man, wise and reserved in his devotion, did not mind laughing at the alleged Apparitions of our Lady. As for Peyramale, who afterwards defended her so bravely, he called the revelations of the visionary "a little carnival of apparitions," and for his own conversion demanded the rather stupid proof of the blossoming of a honeysuckle tree in mid-winter.

Each of them was playing his part, and they were quite right in refusing to accept the heavenly origin of the visions outright. It was better so. To this suspicion we owe the long inquiries, the researches and checks of all sorts, the results of which were so demonstrative that all these unbelieving priests were converted and that, on January 18, 1862, Mgr. Laurence issued a charge in which he declared that "The Apparitions bore all the marks of truth, and that the faithful were justified in regarding them as certain."

This was the beginning of the great pilgrimages. The Virgin's command: "I want people to come here in processions" was about to be fulfilled, and she gave her approbation to the terms of the charge and sanctioned it by setting thereto the seal of her many miracles.

XIII

JUST for this afternoon Lourdes is apparently empty; the great pilgrimages from the country have departed; there remain only the Dutch, the English and a few Flemish people, and what they here call "hamper pilgrimages"—that is to say, bands of peasants on pleasure parties from the surrounding country.

All of these together scarcely amount to more than a few thousand people; this means the peace of the desert for such a place as Lourdes, but tomorrow everything will be as it was before; the *Journal de la Grotte* tells us that there will be monster arrivals of trains from all parts of the country; our rest will be but brief.

I take advantage of this to go to the Grotto to assist at this morning's Mass for the sick. From afar, through the bars of the iron railing, at the back of the hollow, appears the vision of a human being clothed in gold against the fiery background as he officiates.

The Mass has begun. I take my seat beneath the trees on the end of a bench; in front of me are all the ambulances of the patients. Nights seem interminable to the suffering and darkness accentuates the intensity of their ills. How impatiently must they have awaited the dawn in the dormitory where the passing footsteps of the infirmarians were muffled with groans. Will they be cured today? And they count the days towards the end of their stay at Lourdes. Just two or three more; then, if they have not recovered, another climb up another steep of Calvary hill, for they will have to bear the painful rattle and shake of the railway-train. Anxiety increases with the passing of each day; there lie all these poor people, engrossed in telling their beads, suddenly flinging the beseeching glances of a dying animal towards the Virgin, who yonder stands up impassible in the gothic hollow of the rock.

All these poor infirm creatures are unable to move in their ambulances, and respectfully close their eyes when the bell rings for the elevation, and those who can do so join their hands together.

And there is a heart-rending exhibition of suffering and fervour when the time for communion comes. Oh! the unbounded eloquence of their looks when the priest emerges from the Grotto, with the ciborium in his hands, to communicate the bed-ridden one by one!

Not an eye is to be seen in the field of pale faces, nothing but the white veils of eyelids, when the celebrant has returned to the Grotto to communicate through the iron rails, now provided with a cloth, the sick who are well enough to walk and the faithful who are in good health.

Of a truth God's condescension towards those of his flock whose bodies are on the verge of death is most touching; but, Lord, I would have something more! Thou hast said: "Come unto me, all ye who are heavy-laden, and I will relieve you." They have come and they are there; keep thy promise, grant them relief!

And then, remember that if we try to enter into the incomprehensible mystery of thy Blood, we may almost dare to remind thee, O Saviour of the world, that we too, once upon a time, saved thee!

We grope our way, straying through the dimness and hardly discerning amidst our fugitive gleams the unfathomable enigmas of thy Blood; we see that from the day of his birth man gravely offended thee in Eden, and that in order to expunge that offence he had to commit a still greater one; in order to make compensation for the crime of disobedience, he had to become a deicide and not to shrink from a murder beyond compare, to spill the Blood of his God to enable his God to redeem him.

And this Blood that we have helped to give thee for our souls' salvation, we were the first to shed it for the salvation of thy body, for the Innocents were slain in thy stead by Herod!

Here was a substitution of children; all the newborn of Bethlehem paid for the New-born who had fled for refuge to Egypt; thousands of little innocents, fourteen thousand according to the Canon of the Mass of the Abyssinians and the Greek Kalendar, were sacrificed for only one.

And that is a debt—a debt incurred by the Child Jesus which we can claim from the Man-God here, where more than anywhere else blood flows from inward lesions and outward wounds! But perhaps it were fitting for children to pray at the Grotto for the sick, to clamour their invocations in the piscinas, to take their stand as creditors of blood, at Lourdes!

And I recall the desperate processions when God refuses to hear and remains deaf, when the assault of the suppliants breaks down. Here, as at the end of a lost battle, we ought to fling forward our Old Guard, and our Old Guard should be made up of the irresistible phalanx of children's prayers!

But in any case, O Lord, now when the Mass is over and these poor creatures have finished their thanksgivings and are going to be taken back to the hospital, remember that when the ungodly mocked thee on thy way to Calvary, a man was found who had pity on thee and helped thee to bear thy cross. Be thou, now, the Cyrenean to the bed-ridden, and help the life-lorn to bear theirs!

I know not if God has at least ameliorated the state of these sick folk this morning, but certainly he has not healed them after their communion, for I see them still in their ambulances, on returning to the Grotto this afternoon.

They are still there, but now other little wheeled chairs, hitherto unobserved by me, have also taken up their places before the Virgin.

Two of them hold little children, two boys paralysed from the waist to the feet and looked after by their mother, a lady from Ecuador; and from time to time she rises from her stool and seizes the two little ones and flings them on to her back; they look like two little grimacing monkeys, and their living heads wobble to the one side on their mother's shoulder, and their dead legs to the other side over her bosom. She thus takes them to the Grotto and makes them kiss the rock where it has been worn greasy by many mouths, and then puts them back in their carriages, in which they laugh and play. They have only arrived a few days ago, and the lady does not want to go away till they are cured. Will they be?

I cannot help thinking about her. I fancy that in her own country everyone must have blamed her when they saw her undertaking such a costly and lengthy journey. If, after all this fatigue and expense, she returns empty-handed, it will really be terrible, for everyone who has what is called common sense will exult in her discomfiture and laugh at her.

And then the sadness of having hoped for so much and of receiving so little—the regret of going away and saying to herself that perhaps, if she had waited longer, the Virgin would have been touched at last! It is enough to drive anyone mad! But no. Even if our Lady does not answer her prayers, She will give her, as She has done to others, and more freely than to others, in exchange for all her faith, patience and courage; She will make good her defeat by granting her other graces!

All the same, how much I should like heaven to take pity on the distress of this unhappy woman!

And now the Grotto is sweetly peaceful in its disencumbrance; the fireman is tidying up all round the candles; he comes and goes and sets up little bouquets of lights, taking down others whose last leaves of smoke are flying away; and his cap and face and apron are powdered with a kind of hoarfrost. Birds twitter in the ivy, bending under their light weight the branches of honeysuckle hanging beneath the Virgin's feet. The desiccated crutches dance and bump together on their piece of iron wire; a few peasant women, after pressing the shiny olive hued rock with their kisses, themselves impale their modest candles on the spiked stands or place a bouquet in a corner of the Grotto; outside, everyone is saying the rosary, and they step aside respectfully to make room for Mgr. Schoepfer, who also takes advantage of the present calm to come and pray in peace. He goes to the ambulances, talks to the sick, blesses the urchins from Ecuador, and, refusing the prie-dieu offered him by a lady, kneels on the ground and says his rosary just like the others; then he extricates himself from the devout women who encircle him to kiss his ring and returns to the somewhat sorry residence in which he is staying, behind the Rosary.

Yes, Our Lady of Lourdes is surely exorable and gracious and one has a sense of relief and joy in invoking her, but nevertheless in this place I feel a sort of stranger and intruder in Her eyes; I fancy I am calling on someone who is busy and whom I disturb; and the delightfully shadowy crypt of Chartres cathedral occurs to me, an early morning in the little silent vault where it seemed so good to be near Her.

At Lourdes I take part in a public reception, in an official ceremony at which the invited guests file past in batches before the Queen and make their bow; at Chartres, you are alone with Her in a closed chamber, and here you get a commonplace audience in the open-air.

In Paris even, at Notre-Dame des Victoires, at Saint-Séverin, at the black Virgin's with the Dames of St Thomas of Villanova, one is more at home oneself and more at home with Her; at any rate one gets a little dimness and silence; clearly such feelings of intimacy depend upon temperament and upon the kind of piety connected with it, but it must be said that, after taking these differences into account, the Madonna with her diversity of effigies and dwelling-places puts herself within the reach of all; she welcomes the solitaries here and the crowds there; and, after all, everyone can find her according to his needs and tastes.

Most assuredly, this glorious Virgin who is so entirely modern, and who has defined herself by an abstraction, is not the One whom I prefer. I hope, indeed, that She will forgive me in this, for She knows that I love Her in other places and in other forms; and yet is this the way to speak, for how can one escape being gripped by Her whose love was never so strongly asserted towards the suffering members of her Son as in this town?

And I recall the coincidences between certain of the Apparitions to Bernadette and certain feasts and offices, and I think that these conjunctions, willed by Her, afford one more proof of the importance in the divine plan of the much despised Liturgy, which is nevertheless the marrow of the Church herself.

Thus, the first time that She showed herself in the Grotto in a halo of glory was on Thursday, February 11, 1858. Now on that day in the diocese of Tarbes

214

they were celebrating the feast of the Patroness of Shepherdesses. Consequently, Lourdes had that morning said the Mass and recited the Office of St Genevieve, who was also the Patroness of Paris, of the city whence our Lady had come to settle at Lourdes.

Is not the choice of this feast, from the date of which the Virgin spoke at intervals for eighteen days with Soubirous' daughter, significant? Not only does it imply an affectionate regard for the capital and for her sanctuary of Notre Dame des Victoires, but it confirms the predilection of Christ and of his Mother for the people who are most closely connected with the soil, for the country-folk who have followed, far from the centres of civilisation, the biblical calling of the Patriarchs, for the shepherds and shepherdesses of whom Bernadette was one.

And here we may note that the two best-known persons of the nineteenth century, so far as sanctity is concerned, the Blessed Curé d'Ars and Don Bosco, the founder of the Salesians, were also tenders of flocks in their childhood.

On consulting the Ordo of the diocese of Tarbes for 1858, one also finds other coincidences which deserve to be noted.

For instance: the first time that the Virgin ordered prayers for sinners to be made was on Quadragesima Sunday, and this Mass of the First Sunday in Lent in its collects constantly begs God to pardon our sins, and invites us, by the voice of the Evangelist, to expiate by dint of corporal penances the ever-increasing evil of our faults, and, like Christ in the desert, to resist the assaults of the devil and the perpetually renewed temptations of the senses.

The Wednesday on which She thrice cried "Penance!" and the Friday of the same week in which she bade Bernadette to kiss the ground, were the Wednesday and Friday of Ember-week, especially dedicated to the practice of penance. They are, indeed, days of abstinence and fasting and humiliation, and the Church is Careful to have it notified after the Postcommunions of the Masses when the priest says to the faithful: "Bend down your heads unto God."

Hence, all these injunctions by our Lady accord with the Feria of the Proper; She does but repeat and emphasise the notifications of the Office of the day.

Further, at the end of the Masses celebrated the day after this Thursday, February 25, on which She pointed out the place of the spring in the Grotto, the Gospel of St John was read, which tells the story of the paralytic waiting for someone to help him to go down into the Probatica piscina, which was stirred by an angel, so that he might be healed.

It was, in fact, the Gospel of the Friday in Ember-week, which Feria was replaced in the diocese of Farbes by the adventitious feast of the Lance and Nails.

Was not this reminder across the ages of the pool of Bethsaida, which appears to prefigure that of Lourdes, a sort of promise of the miracles which the Virgin was preparing, although she had said nothing about them to Bernadette?

Nevertheless, I cannot help thinking, with regard to this, of how Jesus did not help the young man to dip in the piscina, but merely, said to him: "Arise, and take up thy bed and walk," thus leading the way to the cures without the use of water, which he so often works here today!

We may further remark that, despite all the entreaties of Bernadette, the Virgin only revealed to her that she was the Immaculate Conception on the very day of Christendom's feast of the Annunciation. There is no need to dwell upon the connection between the immaculate origin of the Mother and the immaculate conception of the Son. Although the two Catholic celebrations do not meet in the Church's calendar, now for once only, overleaping the month that comes between them, they are conjoined at Mary's voice in the Grotto of Lourdes.

Finally, the last Apparition to Bernadette took place on Friday, July 16, the feast of Our Lady of Mount Carmel, formerly venerated in the town, in which an altar surmounted by an old retable was already dedicated to her in the old church.

She took her leave on that one of her feast-days in which the Liturgy expresses in her name the sweetest of appeals, the tenderest of assurances. See the Epistle in her Mass: "Come over to me, all ye that desire me, and be filled with my fruits; . . . He that hearkeneth to me shall not be confounded, and they that work by me shall not sin. They that make me known shall have life everlasting."

This indeed is my desire, O Blessed Virgin! In the meantime, the ambulances are returning in single file and the pilgrims are making for the Basilica, where there is to be a sermon; I am almost alone. How much more intimate is the Grotto now! The mischief is that it has to be so administrative with its captured spring, now hidden like any common water in pipes, with its iron railings, like those of a public garden, and its blue enamel slabs, like those of our street-corners, on which in embossed white letters are written *Entrée* on one side and *Sortie* on the other.

One must make a mental effort to think of it as wild and as free as it was in the days of Bernadette, when the river bathed its edges, when moss and grass instead of asphalt gladdened its soil with rosy lilac and pale yellow flowerets of cardamine and golden saxifrage, which blossomed more abundantly than other plants in the ever damp and sunless ground, silted up with ooze when the Gave was in flood.

All these herbs and flowers, except the honeysuckle at the Virgin's feet, are dead in this hollow cave darkened with the smoke of wax-candles.

No one can deny that these changes of appearance and the arrangement of notices and the iron railings have been a necessary consequence of the crowds flocking hither. The same is true of the landscape, of the surroundings, of the Gave, which has had to be thrust farther away, and of the Esplanade; but then, if we look at the question from this point of view, it is only right to say at once that Lourdes must be refashioned from top to bottom.

As a practical man, Père Sempé had admirably organised the quarters of the new town; but at that time he could not foresee the wonderful extension of the pilgrimages; he had marked out gardens and lawns, set up shelters, put benches under the trees, and installed conveniences on all sides; nowhere, in truth, were the needs of the multitude in the performance of their evolutions better provided for, but not for multitudes of over forty-five thousand people! Today, during the weeks of the huge caravans, everything appears to be inadequate, the churches, the shelters, the sanitary arrangements and the seats; especially the space between the Grotto and the Gave is too narrow; the parapet along the river might easily be set farther back to get room, but what would be the good of it? Who can foretell the future? Who knows what Lourdes will be someday?

On the other hand, it is also well to note that the clinic, as it is organised today, is overflooded at such times as these.

When the national pilgrimage arrives, it is only half as bad, for the people to be put up are numbered and checked beforehand; all their identification papers and medical certificates are ready. The same is true of the Belgian pilgrimages which bring practitioners with them, and all their sick are provided with certificates which have been verified and can be counted on with confidence; but when the great provincial pilgrimages are in question!

Dr. Boissarie and Dr. Cox are obliged to put up with papers sent in by no one knows what sort of medicasters, often purposely badly drawn up so as not to compromise themselves as soon as they knew that a request was being made to them for the undertaking of a journey to Lourdes; here there is nothing to rely on; one cannot reckon upon the science or the good faith of such a country Diafoirus;[1] and the clinic has often to hold its tongue in cases which might possibly be interesting. Remedies have been sought for such instances of uncertainty and confusion, but all the solutions hitherto put forward have been found useless upon due reflection.

The best plan would be to have a medical office established in the hospital to verify the certificates and state of health of the patients on arrival, and in some cases to have recourse to X-rays in properly fitted operating rooms. Yes, but how is such a medical council to be composed, for they might hardly ever agree, and how could they personally make a thorough examination of the batches of cripples who occasionally stay for only one day at Lourdes? These would have to be prevented from bathing and perhaps from being cured, until they had passed through the doctors' hands, and that would be impossible!

Zola said that the wounds and sores should be photographed; but photography does not show their colour or give what is below the surface; hence it would afford no guarantee of itself.

No; the most desirable innovation, in my opinion, would be to put up the sick who had found some relief or were on the way to health for a certain time in the hospitals.

As a matter of fact, all of them go away after a few days with the pilgrimages which brought them. They interrupt, if one may say so, the treatment which the

---

1 *Diaforus*, a "medicaster" in Molière's *La malade imaginaire*.

Virgin has begun. And who can tell whether fresh dippings in the piscinas and fresh prayers at the Grotto might not hasten the return of health and prevent relapse, if required?

The clinic, too, would gain from not being compelled to be satisfied with summary examinations, and from being able to study the mode of cure more closely.

Nevertheless, all this would hinder them from attesting many of the marvels, which are really such, as proved, since they must always be officially ignorant of some of the cures wrought at Lourdes. The bed-ridden who have not come with a pilgrimage and who are staying at hotels are often not at all anxious, after their cure, to be cross-questioned and handled in public so as to become regarded in the town as if they were queer animals, and they take their departure without setting foot in the Medical Office. And we may parenthetically observe that this shows how delusive and inaccurate are all the statistics of the cures effected at Lourdes.

Therefore it is all a question of more or less, and hence it matters little whether the Medical Office be rather more or rather less scientifically organised; in substance, its true and only use is not to lose sight of the lives of a certain number of the miraculously healed whose antecedents it knows, whom it has examined immediately after their cure and continues to examine year after year. If no relapse occurs, it can pronounce with certainty: without it, there is no binding certainty. No one, indeed, can boast of having witnessed a miracle at Lourdes, since many an extraordinary cure fails to stand the proof of time, and no real miracle has occurred, in the strict sense of the word, if the disease has only become dormant and wakes up again.

And then, suppose a more reliable method of verification is discovered than that of the certificates, what would be the good of it? If the Virgin raised a man from the dead tomorrow, the freethinkers would cry out on all the house-tops that it was a case of lethargy and that the man had never died; in fact, there will always be a sort of psychical process enabling biased minds still to deny the evidence with what amounts to a kind of good faith.

This evening we are to have a procession; the small number of patients will all go into the vat of the Rosary. I shall just take my stand behind the ambulances and the sick who are seated on the benches. Apart from the little Dutch urchin in his green Tyrolese hat, who always looks like a frog on his back, and the two little brothers from Ecuador whose mother moves me to pity, I have no sick favourites left whose cure I specially desire. All those gathered together in the circle are bedridden people previously to be seen at the Grotto, cases of paralysis and consumption, and others affected with invisible complaints of which I know nothing.

About four o'clock, I take my place behind two young women of the people, Flemish girls with pale and puffy cheeks and both seated, but as I lean over them I inhale such a sickly whiff that I decamp. Will these poor girls be set free from the hidden evil revealed by that frightful odour? I move farther away near some inodorous blind men engaged in prayer.

Preceded, as usual, by beadles and choir-boys, the small procession comes in singing hymns. A bishop is carrying the monstrance, and he is followed by the long-haired prelate from Palestine and the customary band of surpliced priests and the stretcher-bearers.

And here there is something new. Today the invocations are shouted in all languages, first in French, then in English, and afterwards in Dutch and Flemish.

Priests of various nationalities, all in soutanes except the Englishman in a frock coat, follow one another, to vociferate them in the middle of the circus.

The effect is lamentable; you can hear hardly any voices following; those around are silent, for they do not understand a word of what is uttered. Would it not be much more simple to call out the invocations in the Church's own tongue, in Latin?

And then what does it all mean? The cross-channel tourists are but a handful; they have brought two or three ailing persons along with their luggage, and so we have to speak to God in English. Really, this is quite out of proportion!

However, the Blessed Sacrament begins to bless the sick; but somehow I fancy myself present at the shabby rehearsal of a great drama; this all but taciturn facsimile, on so reduced a scale, of the immense processions of bellowing crowds moves one to pity; no one prays with zest and the bed-ridden seem disconcerted and hopeless of being cured. Not a soul writhes before the ostensory. All lower their heads when the shouts of Babel die away on the Esplanade and in the hills without an echo.

Far away I see the two monkeys from Ecuador laughing and their mother saying Paternosters, and the Dutch batrachian lying on his litter, inanimate; not one is any better; this is earth's failure and heaven's fiasco!

To make matters worse, a touch of comedy comes. Just when the Blessed Sacrament reaches my side a layman, walking before it with a white umbrella, makes imperious gestures to an urchin who is tossing himself about but standing. As the boy still fidgets about, he flies into a rage, and there is no end of a bother to make him understand that the child is afflicted with St Vitus's dance and cannot kneel down; and now I note that the Oriental bishop, with his Jesus Christ's head, doubtless convinced that our Lord's blessing is insufficient to save the sick, supplements it with his own!

The round comes to an end, and all scatter in different directions. The Dutch alone remain, and they have to leave Lourdes tonight. They ascend the steps of the Rosary and make groups with the sick in front of them, and the little gnome in his litter is in the middle of them. Alas, he will leave the place uncured! The photographer puts everyone in his right place. The young Dutch girls laugh like mad; the violet-sashed chamberlains do their utmost to keep them in position. You hear the exclamation," Don't move!" and then, it is like the dispersal of a flock of birds; all fly away. What a tale they will have to tell to their girlfriends when they are back in their homes overhanging the canals in which they are reflected in the melancholy background of placid Holland!

I betake myself to the clinic. A few priests are sitting there and cheerily watching a Portuguese who, with his hands tied together, is jumping over chairs, and then bends backwards and almost touches the ground with the nape of his neck.

"A real clown!" says Dr. Boissarie without taking his eyes off him, and when the young fellow has left he tells me that the man's arms and legs were paralysed and that he had started in a railway invalid-carriage from Lisbon for Paris, where he wanted to get medical advice. He felt urged, he never clearly knew why, to turn aside and stop at Lourdes, and there, after a bath in the piscina, he regained the extraordinary suppleness of which he had just given us a demonstration. Then, instead of going to Paris, by way of thanksgiving to the Virgin he decided to settle here to work as a stretcher-bearer and bath-attendant.

"As for his affliction, we have no need to trouble ourselves about it," continues the Doctor; "we know nothing of its antecedents and causes; his paralysis may very well have had a nervous origin . . ."

"But anyhow," breaks in a priest who is arranging his notes, "the doctors who looked after him could not cure him; it would be presuming too far to believe that the Parisians would have succeeded where their Portuguese colleagues failed. Why then did the Blessed Virgin work no miracle when it was a case of nervous affection, which is often far more incurable than many another? The eternal argument of neurosis used by free-thinkers does not seem to me at all decisive . . ."

"Well, it is not at all clear," observes another Abbé; "why anyone who happens to be afflicted with nerves should be deprived of favours granted to those who are not."

"Quite so; but what is the use of arguing?" cries the doctor; "none are so deaf as those who won't hear. If only our opponents were always men of good faith; but just listen to this; it will enlighten you as to the mentality of some of the unbelievers.

"One day we were examining the case of a sick woman who produced a doctor's certificate showing that she was consumptive—and so she was. After taking a bath she was cured and all her lesions disappeared. For fear of any mistake being made, we telegraphed to the doctor—but said nothing about the cure—and asked him if his patient, who was one of long standing, was really consumptive, and he answered us 'yes,' confirming the nature of her malady by his telegram.

"As soon as she got home, the woman went to see the doctor, who was astonished, sounded her, cross-examined her, and made her come to see him three times before agreeing to give her a certificate of being cured. But then, as it was a question of a miraculous cure of Lourdes, he declared in this document that his patient had never had anything but an ordinary cold!"

The heat in the little office is terrible. I leave it along with an ecclesiastic who says to me:

"Dr. Boissarie is right. Why should we argue with people who, when confronted with a miracle, nevertheless try to find natural causes to account for it and make use of grand words which they will no doubt find as hard to explain as Zola did when he spoke of 'nutrimental trouble' in connection with lupus? The case of Gabriel Gargam is typical, and here to the point. I believe you know his cure, for I have several times seen you talking to him. . . ."

"Yes, I knew him at the piscinas; he is an intelligent man, both humble and charming."

"Very well. I will summarise his story in a few words so that you may the sooner appreciate the madness of the notions it suggests to unbelievers. He was a travelling clerk in the postal service. On December 17, 1899, his carriage was coupled on to the express from Bordeaux to Paris. Through a breakdown of the engine the train came to a standstill near Angoulême and was run into by an express travelling at sixty miles an hour. The Post Office carriage was smashed to pieces, and Gargam was hurled about twenty yards from the rail into the snow.

"There he was picked up next morning and carried to the hospital at Angouléme in a dying condition. He was covered with wounds, his collar-bone was broken, and he was paralysed from his waist to his feet. He could not swallow anything, and soon, even with a probe made use of several times a day, to nourish him became all but impossible.

"A suit was started against the Orleans Railway Company. Doctors were called in to make their reports, and all of them concluded that the case was incurable and must end fatally sooner or later. In view of these reports the Company, which at first had offered to pay a pension of three thousand francs, was ordered by the sentence of the court of Angoulême to pay one of six thousand, as well as an indemnity of sixty thousand francs.

"You will observe that if ever a patient was carefully examined it was this man, and if the doctors of the Orleans Railway Company, who would have been glad in the interests of their clients to pronounce him curable, declared that he was done for, he must really have been so.

"The prognosis was, moreover, right. Gargam's state grew worse. One day they noticed that his feet were black; it was thought that they were dirty, but as soon as they touched his skin to clean them, it broke and humour ran out. It was gangrene too.

"Gargam had no faith at all, but his family had, and prayed for him with fervour. Medical science owned that it was powerless even to give relief, and they decided to take him to Lourdes. He allowed this to be done so as not to drive his mother to despair, but he did not at all expect to be cured. He was placed upon a special litter provided with a mattress, which was hoisted into the train. A short time before arriving at the Lourdes station his mother pointed out to him the great crucifix on the hill of the Stations of the Cross and begged him to kiss his hand to it or at least to bow to it.

"He refused, and turned his head away.

"Having brought him in his litter to the piscinas, he was slipped into the bath while everyone was at prayer. He fainted, then opened his eyes and stood straight up. This man, after being worn out with twenty months of sickness and reduced to the state of a skeleton, walked.

The gangrene had vanished and his feet were now well. He was no longer paralysed and, though for the last few days his stomach no longer could endure the passage of the probe, it now easily digested all kinds of food; one may say that Gargam had risen from the dead at a stroke."

"Yes, and what strikes me most is this, that he had not the faith, or at least, if he had it, it was in a forgotten state, being altogether gone since his childhood. From all the talks I had with him, he appears to me to have been the subject of a twofold miracle: he believed at the same moment as he was cured; both occurred spontaneously at the same instant. What then becomes of the faith that auto-suggests the patient beforehand, the curative faith of Charcot?"

"I don't know; but contrarily to the diagnosis of the chief house-surgeon of the Angoulême hospital, who attributed Gargam's paralysis to an increasingly diseased marrow, the infidels declared immediately after the miracle that this paralysis must have had a nervous origin."

"And what about the origin of the gangrene? Was it, too, nervous?"

"I don't think so," said the Abbé with a laugh; "but suppose they are right about the nature of the disease, they still have to explain the instantaneous cure of the gangrene, the restoration of strength without convalescence after a year of exhaustion, and the recovery of the stomach in a moment."

"Well, they will reply that these are the effects of the shock produced by the cold water, the benefits of hydrotherapeutic reaction. Only, if they believe in the power of such therapeutics, why the devil don't they resort to it in similar cases in Paris? You can practise hydrotherapy elsewhere than here, and even better than here; for, after all, there is no bathing establishment worse equipped than that of Lourdes, since it possesses nothing in the way of apparatus but baths of dirty water.

"And while they are about it, they might as well try to explain the piscina system, in which women are bathed without worrying about their condition or whether they have finished their digestion. I should be very interested to know what results such treatment would yield in the nervous affections of the women patients at La Salpêtrière for instance!"

XIV

I BEGIN to feel rather tired. Empty yesterday, Lourdes is again full; the noisy roll of the *Ave Marias* is resumed; and for the last three weeks I have been looking in daily at the hospital and clinic, exercising the misty functions of a medical student. Now there are no more outrageous cases; nightmare faces such as that of the peasant from Coutances, larva-heads like the woman's whose eye flourished about, like a slug's, on the end of a tentacle. Excepting an old man of a pearly grey tinge, which reminds me of certain workmen employed in tobacco factories, all the new-comers at the hospital are patients unembellished by any special horror, having no peculiar stamp. I have seen so many of their kind that I no longer loiter round the beds. Living here, you end, upon my word, by losing all your interest in current maladies, and don't get excited by anything but runaways from leper-asylums and monstrosities. You are gripped with the giddiness of excesses; I understand this since the unpacking of bestiaries is over; but what I feel most just now is the need of not having to move, of not having to inhale the mingled whiffs of dust and

231

vanilla and suppuration which make up the sigillated scent of Lourdes.

From my window the spectacle of the new town lying at the bottom of its basin of hills hardly arouses me to enthusiasm. Is it because I come on my father's side from a fiat sea-bound land? But plainly I have less and less feeling for the mountains; indeed, they strike me as a sort of congealed ocean; the only life they have is due to a trick of the sky; the clouds passing over the peaks play the part of dumb waves, leaping on and curling their dry crests of foam; without these there would be absolute immobility, an earth lying dead and sterile through extremes of cold. The worst of it is that though these mountains are very high, they do not appear at all lofty, nor do they suggest any idea of the infinite, but a sense of being stifled. Well, certainly I wouldn't give a penny to be an Alpinist. The absurd ascents people make, as everybody knows, with their calves enswathed in strips of Scotch wool and alpine-stock in hand, make but little appeal to me. My imagination is quite strong enough for me, while still sitting in an armchair, to bring before my mind horizons the immensity of which far outstrips that which extends from the mountain-tops; the beautiful is less what one sees than what one dreams, and I admit that my dream was of a very different Lourdes; but after all, since I am here, I must confess that Nature stirs me more by her breadth than by her height, and that the melancholy crossing of the Landes, with the sunsets fading away in the long stretches of the pine-woods, affects me far otherwise than does this shortened scenery of ridges and glaciers.

In any case, I am tired of pilgrims and weary of landscapes; so today I stay at home in my room and run over books on the copies of Lourdes which have been set up in Belgium and Turkey.

And I say to myself that Our Lady of Lourdes is truly disconcerting, for the copies are as good as the original, and sometimes are even more fertile and active in the production of miracles.

In Belgium, the story of the sanctuary of Oostaker in a small town in the middle of Slootenclriesch Park, two and a half miles from Ghent, is singular, to say the least of it. It started with a worldly project with which the Virgin had nothing to do. In 1870 the taste for aquariums was all the fashion among wealthy Belgians; a Marchioness de Courtebourne, who owned the château of Slootendriesch, took it into her head to build one, and as no aquarium can do without a sham grotto, she decided to have one erected. When the site had been selected in her park, the Work was begun. Thereupon the Abbé Moreels, the rector of Oostaker, displays an image of the Grotto at Lourdes to the Marchioness and gets her to reserve a nook in her cemented pile of rocks for a statue of the Immaculate Conception, modelled on that in the Pyrenees. All was finished in 1871; and three years afterwards, the few peasants from the village who used to come to pray at the aquarium before the Virgin had given rise, no one quite knows how, to an influx of thousands of visitors. They came at last to ten thousand in one day, and there was an outburst of miracles.

The first one to be recorded occurred on February 12, 1874; and it happened to Matilda Verkimpe, a child

233

of ten living at Loochristi. She was lame, and could not walk without crutches; all the doctors of Ghent had declared that they could do nothing to cure her. Her mother went to the Grotto to pray for her cure, bringing back some of the Lourdes water which was distributed there, and rubbed her daughter's leg with the water during a novena. At the end of the novena, the little girl was instantaneously cured and was able to go on foot to give thanks to the Virgin.

And the miracles go on. The usual practice is to go round the Grotto three times, to wash with the water dropping from a basin belonging to the aquarium, into which a few drops from the spring at Lourdes are thrown every morning, and the most various diseases, such as coxalgia and blindness, disappear as soon as the water touches them.

In the month of May of 1875, to meet the needs of the pilgrims they erected a gothic church without a transept and with two towers; they entrusted the service of the pilgrimages to the Jesuits of the Belgian Province, and Oostaker became famous throughout Flanders. Thousands of candles are burnt there, just as at Lourdes, and there are pyramids of ex-votos over the Grotto amidst the trees.

It was here that occurred the most unheard-of cure that has ever been witnessed in the memory of man.

On February 16, 1867, a peasant named Pierre de Rudder, living in the village of Jabbeke, near Bruges, had his left leg broken by the fall of a tree; the tibia and fibula were fractured, and so numerous were the fragments of bone that you could hear them rattling together like nuts in a bag, to use the words of the doctor who first attended the case. When the pieces were taken out of the tissues, the two bones that remained intact could be seen in the wound over an inch apart.

At that time antiseptic treatment was unknown, and stout bandages were used in vain, for the two bones were swimming in pus and could never be brought to unite together; the lower part of the limb was no longer attached to the other, and swung in all directions like a rag.

Surgeon after surgeon pronounced the case incurable, and Professor Thiart of Brussels, who was consulted in the last resort, advised the amputation of the leg.

De Rudder refused this; and for more than eight years he suffered fearful torture, having to dress the wound several times a day since it kept on discharging, and dragging himself along, as best he could, on crutches.

He had heard about Oostaker, and resolved to get there and ask the Virgin to cure him. On April 7, 1875, he was lifted into the train for Ghent by three men. On arriving there he was driven in the Oostaker omnibus, and though his leg was well wrapped up, it discharged streams of blood and pus, which leaked through the linen bandages and streaked the seat. On reaching the Virgin's statue, he rested a little, drank a mouthful of water, and wanted to make the tour of the Grotto three times like the other pilgrims. Supported by a woman, he got round twice, and, having no strength left, fell on to a seat quite exhausted. He implored Our Lady of Lourdes to save him and suddenly lost his senses, not knowing where he was, but on coming to himself found that he was kneeling in front of Her, and got up cured. There was no gap left and his bones had united; he did not even limp, for both his legs were the same length.

This prodigy caused an immense sensation throughout Flanders. Twenty-eight doctors took the case in hand; they made the most minute enquiries, superintended by both Catholics and unbelievers for the sake of greater impartiality; they cross-questioned all the practitioners who had attended him, all the villagers of Jabbeke who had witnessed the state of his wound on the day of his departure, all who had been present at the miracle; they subjected De Rudder to the strictest examination; people had to admit the authenticity of the unprecedented fact of the spontaneous cure of a wound in a moment and of the instantaneous growth of a piece of bone over an inch long to fill up the gap where it was wanting, following upon a prayer.

On the leg, just where it was broken, remained merely a bluish spot, as if meant to testify that there was no illusion and to show that the fracture had really occurred.

Twenty years passed away without any weakening of his leg or its becoming any less sound than the other one, and De Rudder died of pneumonia at the age of seventy-five on March 22, 1898. On May 24 of the following year an autopsy of the leg was made.

You remark that our Lady does not risk any misses, as they say in billiards; She restored the leg as the most skilful of surgeons might have done, had the operation been possible; and She made it possible by getting rid of a suppurating wound immediately, and by the instantaneous creation of a bone.

Assuredly this autopsy on a miracle is the most extraordinary proof that could possibly have been given of supernatural action intervening for the relief of man's helplessness in an earthly cure. The "nervous" wounds of Zola, autosuggestion, curative faith, and all the old fudge of La Salpêtrière and Nancy are thus knocked out at a single blow.

There is no way out, here. As Dr. Boissarie well says in the *Annales de Notre-Dame de Lourdes:* "It may be said that the doctors did not lose sight of De Rudder for thirty-two years; with unflagging persistence they waited for his death to make an autopsy to find out by what procedure God could indeed cure a fractured leg. Thanks to the materials collected by them, the cure of De Rudder will remain a model of what can be achieved by well conducted investigations. Science affords no more conclusive fact."

What may seem strange at first sight is this, that such a miracle, perhaps the plainest man has ever been able to handle and see, should have taken place not at Lourdes itself, but at one of its auxiliaries. Yet the selection is not strange if one reflects thereon. Suppose De Rudder's cure had taken place at Lourdes, the unbelievers would have been eager to deny it; in any case they would have refused to participate in the enquiries despite all the invitations offered them to come and make sure of the verity of the phenomena to be witnessed at the Lourdes clinic.

The few of independent mind who desired to verify and study the cure with their own eyes would perhaps have shrunk from the loss of time and the expense involved by railway travelling in France; in a word, not one of them might have been able to undertake such a task at his own cost.

In Belgium it is otherwise. Journeys in that little country are always inexpensive and short; then there is something in the Belgian temperament which is not to be found in the more highly-strung and eager temperament of the French, something methodical and particular, administrative and even heavy, if they set their heart on it, but incapable of discouragement and of turning aside from the path they have laid down, and it is thanks to these qualities or these defects, if you will, that we have obtained such accurate information as to the case of De Rudder.

The Virgin's choice of a country both phlegmatic and punctilious is therefore intelligible. Let us note further that her Son acted in the same way when he willed to impress upon the world the name of one of his *stigmatisées*,[1] Louise Lateau. He chose her in Flanders and she became the subject of searching investigations and of all sorts of experiments; doctors of every school went to see her in her poor cottage at Bois d'Haine. Louise Lateau is famous all the world over. Who knows anything of another French *stigmatisée* in whom the divine element is, perhaps, as surely traceable? Except a few Catholic doctors such as Dr. Imbert-Gourbeyre,

---

1 *Stigmatisée*, "marked with the stigmata," a woman stamped with the Five Wounds of the Crucified.

who was entrusted by Mgr. Fournier, formerly Bishop of Nantes, with the careful examination and close supervision of her, no medical man has taken any trouble about her during the twenty years she has been confined to her bed; and with the exception of a few people interested in mysticism, no one knows anything of Marie—Julie Jahenny of La Fraudais!

So would it have been with Louise Lateau, had she lived in France rather than in Belgium.

To return to De Rudder, his leg-bones are kept at the University of Louvain, but copper models of them have been given to Lourdes, where they may be seen in the Medical Record Office on Dr. Boissarie's desk.

Such, in few words, is the story of the sanctuary of Oostaker-lez-Gand.

The one which was inaugurated in the suburb of Feri-Keui at Constantinople is easily explained if one remembers how passionately the hyperdulia of our Lady, despite the age-long existence and the many efforts of Mohammedanism, has been and continues to be maintained by the Catholics and schismatics of the Levant.

It is in the East that the cultus of the Virgin was born. According to a very old tradition mentioned by Cardinal de Vitry and the Bollandists, a tradition which also occurs in the revelations of Mary of Agreda, St Peter is said to have founded, even in the Virgin's lifetime, an oratory in her honour in the town of Antarados. This sanctuary is said to have been the first in the world to have been built in her name.

Since then churches dedicated to her name have spread through all the regions of the East, and in the Middle Ages some were so famous that they attracted pilgrimages from all over the world, just as Lourdes does now; and there were two in particular, Our Lady of Tartasus, where, says Joinville, "Our Lord has wrought many a fine miracle in honour of his Mother"—and Our Lady of Saidnaya, where they used to venerate a portrait of the Madonna attributed to St Luke.

And just as the worship of St Joachim's daughter in the Levant preceded our own, so was the cultus of the Immaculate Conception there kept up by the Greeks from the eighth century, while in the West discussion was long continued as to whether this privilege was to be accorded to the Mother of our Lord.

Lastly, nowhere was Mary revered and made much of more persistently and magnificently than in the Liturgies of the East. The Offices of the various Rites overflow with outbursts and enthusiastic cries and fiery praises beside which our Office prayers appear but poor and cold. In addition to the burning transports and the fond hyperbolas of their hymn writers and melodies, even their Masses, which are so dramatic and familiar, celebrate her praises in a manner far beyond anything to be found in ours.

All the Armenian, Maronite and Syriac Masses begin with a prayer personally addressed to her at the foot of the altar by the priest before he begins the *Confiteor*; the Sacrifice is offered under her patronage; in the Coptic Rite they incense her picture during the Holy Mysteries; and as for the Chaldean Rite, it proclaims her mercy and greatness eleven times a day.

Thus the place which She occupies in the Levantine Offices is clearly far more important than in our own; to say nothing of the settled custom in their churches of placing her picture on the altar surrounded with flowers, and of blessing the people with it after the censings and the chanting of the Litanies.

The Virgin is, therefore, an object of adulation and love in these lands, to which, moreover, she belonged, far more than anywhere else, and we can understand her affection for these peoples who were both the first to trust in her and her oldest friends.

Henceforth, it is only natural that She should have admitted them to participate in the graces which She was scattering among the faithful of the West; and if She chose Constantinople to be the dispensary of her benefits, it is perhaps because the fame of her miracles could spread thence most readily throughout Asia Minor, and also perhaps because this was the town in which her perpetual Virginity was defined and proclaimed against the heretics.

In order to organise this auxiliary of Lourdes in Turkey She made use of the most practical and ready means. She did not appear afresh to a new shepherdess nor did she create a new spring, for in an infidel land her apparitions would have aroused storms of fanaticism and stirred up all sorts of disputes; She did not betake herself, but She had herself taken noiselessly from Lourdes to Constantinople, where they knew by hearsay her renown as the miraculous Panagia, and from there her light has shone throughout the Levant.

The way in which her translation from the West to the East came about is one of the simplest.

The Georgian Fathers founded a house at Montanban in 1872 for the education of their novices, and had to leave France in 1880 owing to the decrees of expulsion, and they returned to Constantinople where their convent was installed. On the feast of the Annunciation, March 25, 1881, they dedicated an altar to Our Lady of Lourdes in their chapel, and set above it a statue like the one in the Grotto, and had water from the spring sent them.

This was all that was needed to bring about an immediate rush of astonishing miracles; soon they became so numerous that Cardinal Vincent Vannutelli, then Archbishop of Sardis and apostolic delegate of the Holy See in Turkey, had to set up a commission of inquiry to examine the cures.

Paralysis, epilepsy and cancer disappeared in a twinkling—a Jew of Orta-Keui, who was deaf in both ears, and a child of thirteen, club-footed from birth, were both cured in a moment; but it was mostly the one-eyed or the totally blind who were cured instantaneously; cases of ophthalmia, which are so common and obdurate in the Levant, yielded to a simple lotion and a few prayers. The fame of these extraordinary facts was immense, and people of the most various creeds came to visit the statue of Our Lady of Lourdes in the Georgian Fathers' chapel.

Besides women of every caste, pashas, Turkish officers and soldiers, eunuchs and dervishes mingled with the crowd that invaded the convent. Greeks and Armenians and Bulgarian schismatics, Mohammedans and Jews were cured just as well as Catholics. The

Immaculate Conception seemed to care but little about the difference of creeds and to pay not the slightest attention, so far as temporal favours were concerned, to the axiom "outside the Church there is no salvation." Indeed, She had always acted in this manner, for in 1203, in her sanctuary of Our Lady of Saidnaya, She had miraculously healed Mohammedans and saved the Sultan of Damascus, the brother of Saladin, from a fatal illness, and he determined in his gratitude to maintain a lamp burning perpetually before her ikon in the church. After all, are not all men, whether they be Christians or not, her children, and did not Christ become incarnate to redeem them all?

Finally, since the Catholics in Turkey are but few, the Georgians' chapel would have been a very poor auxiliary of the great pilgrimages of Lourdes, at the best a mere wretched prayer-stall, unless the multitude of Mussulmans and schismatics had also flocked in. And it must indeed have been a strange spectacle to see the processions, made of a mixture of all kinds of creeds, invoking Her whom they call "Meriem-Ana" or "Bikir Meriem," and asking for and obtaining cures by ways even more liturgical than those of Lourdes.

Their procedure, indeed, was as follows:

After the invocations in the chapel at the Virgin's altar, the pilgrims of both sexes went to the sacristy. There they were sprinkled with holy water and had the Gospel read to them; they were then blessed by placing the Holy Gospels upon their heads and were made to kiss the cross which was engraved on the flat part of the book.

And cures were wrought by drinking Lourdes water afterwards, or by rubbing themselves with it or with the oil of the lamps burning before the Madonna's altar in the church.

Sometimes, too, the Mohammedan women would unfold handkerchiefs or shirts meant to be worn, in accordance with Turkish custom, by those whose recovery they were praying for—and, before beginning their invocations, they placed them on the first steps of the altar, and came to fetch them away afterwards.

A few years later they burned from four to five thousand candles in the chapel and distributed considerable quantities of water and medals gratuitously.

From Mesopotamia and Turkestan came requests for it, and—still more strange to say—from Medina and Mecca, the two holy towns of Islam!

Among the cures recognised as such by the Commission of Inquiry is one of special interest because it is a forerunner of one of the famous cures of Lourdes, that of the woman with the needle.

In Dr. Boissarie's clear and careful book, *Lourdes, depius 1858 jusqu' à nos jours*, may be read a detailed account of the woman, whose case he observed and studied very closely; and it may be summed up in a few lines.

Célestine Dubois had had a piece of a broken needle in her hand for seven years. The hand became swollen and the fingers contracted and bent. Incisions were made, and the wound was kept open for three weeks, but they could never get the bit of the needle out.

On August 20, 1886, the woman thrust her hand into one of the piscinas at Lourdes, and the needle, forcing its way through a passage more than three inches long, came out all of itself, after suddenly passing beneath the skin at the top of the thumb.

In November, 1882—that is to say, four years before this happened—a Catholic Armenian of Pera at Constantinople came to the Georgians' chapel with a fragment of a needle in her finger. The surgeons gave up the hope of getting rid of it; inflammation extended from her hand to her arm, and her sufferings were atrocious. This woman made a novena before the altar, and at the end of the novena the needle came out of its own accord and the inflammation subsided.

And what has become of the chapel at Feri-Keui since then? An article in one of the chief papers of Constantinople, the *Stamboul*, tells me that this year (1906) they have celebrated the silver wedding of the sanctuary. The little convent of the Georgian Fathers has been transformed into a huge abbey, but the church remains the same. Thousands of ex-votos cover the walls; crowds of all creeds still flow in, and the Virgin still dispenses her favours there.

Auxiliaries of Lourdes are to be found in other countries, in France, in Italy, in Spain and in Austria. Missionaries have built churches dedicated to her name in America and Oceania, in China and India. Unfortunately, there is no accurate and carefully checked information about any miracles, which are doubtless taking place in them, to be obtained.

XV

THE prospect of getting back to Paris, a singularly quiet place compared with Lourdes in the pilgrimage season, charms me. I feel as if I were returning to some large and kindly country town in which there are still black churches, people who can pray without bawling, and liturgical offices worthy of the name.

And yet, while fastening up my bag, I say to myself: these Pardons of the Pyrenees are well worth seeing, and when the memory of all the pious hustle and of the din of the trombones and of the shouting has faded away, Lourdes will appear to me in the distance as a dream-city in which one lives an intense life in a state of intoxication interrupted with fits of revulsion, but infinitely sweet at times, when the atmosphere seems specially impregnated with the divine breath of healing. The Virgin willed to have crowds, as in the Middle Ages, and She has them. Are they of the same kind? Doubtless the ingenuous spirit and the naïve faith of the old peasant women has hardly changed; the life led by the multitude here, sleeping in the Rosary, eating on the seats and on the patches of grass, recalls that of the mobs of yore, sleeping in Chartres cathedral— the pavement was made sloping so that it could be slushed clean with water next morning—or camping out round the black Virgin, in the open-air, amidst the plains of the Beauce; but everything has grown cheaper and commoner; the magnificence of the cathedral, the charm of the costumes, the ample breadth of the tutelary liturgies, are no more. Lourdes, born yesterday, has been reared in the unwholesome cradle of our times and it exhales the fetid odour of the industries which weigh it down. Once, when one of the Blue Sisters from Beaune, beneath her hennin and splendid fifteenth-century dress, was praying on her knees with arms extended, I was transported by a vision of the ages of yore, but the arrival of the devotees of today, with their made-up faces and their apish antics with powder and paste, their thin fingers running through their rosary-beads, their deadly hats and gowns of funereal soot and ashes, flung me back into my implacable disgust for my own era, and I thought that if it were a salutary thing to visit Lourdes, one must not stay there long, for the dramatic character of the cures which is, at the outset, fearfully thrilling, grows dull in the end, and then the hideousness of all that is around you and of all that meets your eyes becomes dominant.

In fine, the impressions you carry away are of two kinds, and they are reciprocally hostile and irreconcilable.

Lourdes is an immense St Louis Hospital flung forth into a gigantic Neuilly festival; it is an essence of horror spilt drop by drop into a hogshead of coarse mirth; it is alike dolorous and clownish and stupid. Nowhere are such outbursts of debased piety to be found, and fetishism to the point of the Virgin's *poste restante*; and nowhere has the Satanism of ugliness wielded such a vehement and cynical power.

Yes, indeed, all this is very wretched; it urges you to leave the town and never to set foot in it again; but it is the foolish background of a place without compeer; on the face of it, thank God, it is far otherwise.

First of all, there is the faith of the people who are gathered together to invoke the Virgin, a faith that nowhere else breaks forth in such a burning lava-flow; and it never flags. Today our Lady is deaf to all supplications; She turns her face away and says nothing; the crowd shoulders the burden of patience and confines itself to expectation, only to burst out into flaming *Magnificats* when the sick man suddenly rises and is flung upon his feet before the Blessed Sacrament or on leaving the piscina. It is a return to the resolute confidence of the Middle Ages; it is also the fusion of classes mingled together in a single unparalleled love, in a single unparalleled hope.

And then there is the charity which is more highly exalted at Lourdes than anywhere else in the world. For a few fussy self-important persons who look on at others working and deal out to them indiscriminately all sorts of muddled orders, how many are there who sacrifice excursions into the mountains or to the seaside in order to spend their holidays in this place, dragging round ambulances and bathing the sick. Some of them are young and wealthy and could travel more merrily and entertainingly; others are in business and leave their offices for a month to do the work of cab-horses and porters, and these are often the only holidays they can get! How many are the ladies, like the good old woman with the little girl with gangrened feet, who left her relations and her rooms to sleep on a litter and to watch the bedridden at night. And all these people are so taken up and worn out by their work that they cannot find time to go as much as they would wish, like other pilgrims, to pray at the spring alone by themselves; they are harnessed into serving at their own expense.

And even among the visitors who do not toil at the ambulances and piscinas, how many are so moved to pity the poor waifs of humanity they see being drawn along the roads that they entirely forget self and invoke the Madonna with all their might on their behalf. Herein is the good of self-forgetfulness, herein, too, that most rare thing, the love of one's neighbour. The baggage of selfishness has been left behind in the cloakroom; who can say whether it will not weigh lighter when they come to fetch it?

To sum up: at Lourdes you see a renewal of the Gospels; you are in a lazaretto for souls in which you are disinfected with the antiseptic of charity. Compared with these salutary benefits, what is the disorder of folly and ugliness, what the purely human side of the drawbacks?

Lastly, here is the Virgin both compassionate and sweet, and here she seems, at certain moments, to be more loving and nearer to us than she does anywhere else.

And She it is, by her miraculous cures, who has made this place of pilgrimage famous all the world over. The indifferent and the sceptical cannot understand what their reason and their senses cannot grasp, and give no heed to the spiritual graces She pours out in such abundance at the Grotto; they can only be touched by the visible and the palpable, by material prodigies, by the abolition of diseases and wounds; and for them it all amounts to this: first, to ascertain whether cures are really wrought at Lourdes; and then, whether such cures are, as Catholics assert, the entire upsetting of nature's laws, the complete disavowal of all medical methods, the negation of all hygienic rules and scientific forecasts. This is all that interests them.

Throughout this book I believe I have answered these questions with examples. After giving the objections and the replies, all I have to do is to bring them together and to recapitulate them in a few lines.

At the outset, directly after the apparitions to Bernadette, the freethinkers, staggered by the mystery of incomprehensible cures, thought that they could be explained by the therapeutic qualities of the spring; but the water was analysed, and it was recognised that it had no medicinal properties. And then, what magical powers must this water of Youth have possessed, since, in opposition to the specific results produced by all the thermal springs, it cured all sorts of infirmities and diseases alike? It must have been an earthly panacea, one single remedy applicable to a diversity of evils!

Hitherto nature has endowed us with no such myrobalans as this. This once admitted, it was impossible to deny the reality of facts witnessed and observed by thousands of persons, and new reasons had to be discovered. Hence they adopted the theory that the patients were neuropathic, carried away by faith, victims of autosuggestion, who got well because they had the mind and felt that they were certain to be cured.

To give this hypothesis any chance of proving correct, the Virgin ought to have operated solely upon cases of hysteria and neurosis, on those with a monomania for being cured, in fact. But She gets rid of consumption in its last stages, cancer, Pott's disease and gangrene; She sets straight the club-footed, makes the blind to see and the deaf to hear, and treats all sorts of affections, including both organic disorders and wounds. Hence, unless it is boldly asserted that all the ills of humankind, without a single exception, are traceable to some nervous breakdown, the explanation is inadequate.

But I will grant the theory; I will admit that all the cases of gangrene and cancer healed at Lourdes have been cured through some wave of moral feeling, an over-excited imagination, through a powerful desire and the energy of suggestion; and then, can children possibly be cured by the same means?

I have spoken of the urchin from Belley and his wooden gutter. He may have been seven or eight; was he old enough to be hypnotised? I am ready to believe even that; so let us go on to the younger still. In his fully documented book on Lourdes, Abbé Bertrin takes at hazard from the medical records of the clinic the cures of yet younger children—cures, too, that have lasted—Fernand Ballin's cure of a bent knee in 1895 (age, thirty months); Yvonne Aumatre, a doctor's daughter, cured of a double clubbed-foot in 1896 (age, twenty-three months); Paul Marcere's cure of two congenital hernias in 1866, when he was just a year old; and how many others!

Will anyone say that children of their ages could have practised autosuggestion? Why, it would be madness to maintain it.

On the other hand, why should it be supposed that, at Lourdes, the exaltation of faith is the principal means of healing?

Why, then, are so many people with the gift of faith not cured, whereas so many of those who have it not are so? For after all—not to mention the case of Gargam and of very many others, such as that of Lucie Faure of Puylaurens (Tarn), on August 24, 1882, who was convinced of the uselessness of the baths and only bathed in the piscina to please her companions and came forth instantaneously healed of a dislocation of the femur from which she had suffered for twenty-eight years—there are proved cases of those who believed neither in God nor devil and nevertheless have been healed through the prayers of bystanders, such as that of one Kersblick, the blind beggar of Lille, who never set foot inside a church and scoffed at the Virgin of Lourdes!

Then there are others who had faith and nothing happened, however much they whipped it up and stimulated it by prayers and cries at Lourdes; they went away with no hope of any miracle, and then were delivered on reaching home!

In all this, what becomes of the curative faith of Charcot, of the faith that heals, despite her desire not to be healed, the Abbess of the Poor Clares of Lourdes?

And what is the meaning of all that is said by Zola and others, when they assert that the sick are hypnotised by the stage-scenery, by the shock of the cold water, by the lights of the Grotto and the roll of the *Aves?*

The patients are set free from their afflictions—and now most of these cases occur when they are in corners by themselves, without any bathing or drinking of water or being blessed by the Blessed Sacrament, without prayer in common, and without the assistance of the invocations which made such an impression upon Zola.

He speaks of the "healing inspiration of the crowd," of the "unknown power of the crowd." This power—its true name is prayer—is undeniable, but, I say it again, it is no more indispensable for the healing of the sick than are the setting and the surroundings. This is proved by the healing of people in their own homes, without going to Lourdes, after making a simple novena. Lasserre's case, to mention only one, is, from this point of view, typical. At home in Paris he used lotions of water sent him from Lourdes, and suddenly found himself released from the affection of his eyes; and there are others who never resorted even to such means as he used, but who, without stirring from their own rooms, after receiving Holy Communion, have obtained the like favours by merely invoking Our Lady of Lourdes.

Thus people have recovered their health, either here or elsewhere, either with the water or without it, sometimes suddenly, sometimes slowly.

In the latter case, it looks as if the Madonna were very busy, and as if She were satisfied with giving nature a fillip to set her to work, leaving her, when her processes had been once resumed, to finish the cure of her own accord.

And there is the same variety in the ways in which the cures are worked. Some suffer in the process of healing and others do not; some are swept up by the tide and set on their feet, others are seized with shuddering or with hot and cold thrills, while others feel nothing at all; some are conscious of being cured; others, like Madame Rouchel with her lupus, are cured without knowing it; and lastly, others, like her, retain scars and traces of their ulcers, whilst others, like Marie Lemarchand, show none at all! Explain it, if you can. The truth is that there is no set rule, but that the Virgin cures whomsoever, wheresoever and howsoever She wills.

Until these latter days, as I have said, unbelievers replied to the word "Miracle" with the words "Auto-suggestion" and "Curative Faith." At the present time, almost all the freethinking doctors, knowing how limited are the results of therapeutic suggestion, confess that over-excited imagination and self-hypnotism are inadequate causes to solve the problems raised by such prodigies as, for instance, the immediate and abiding elimination of cancer, and they have tried to take their stand on surer ground; but they have confined themselves, as always, to baptising the difficulty with a new name and to discovering a new hole for the ostrich's head, to avoid the sight of any miracle.

They confess that the cures of Lourdes are incomprehensible—yes, of course—but they are due to "still unknown forces of nature," they are "marvels hitherto unexplained," and that is all.

Well then, there must be two forces of opposite and contradictory kinds, for those that are unknown are the direct negation of those that are known; so now we are at once driven into utter inconsistency. For, ever since the world has been what it is, it is certain, it is daily proved by experience, that nature has never been able to close up a wound, even if it were of nervous origin, in a minute; to renew a decayed skin in a second; to dry up—as in De Rudder's case—a suppurating wound and make a new bone grow in place of another while there is just time enough to say a prayer. It is quite as surely settled that she has never been able to restore in a flash, without the least suspicion of convalescence, a constitution ruined by long illness and inanition; and here, all of a sudden, there intervene unknown forces acting in a manner which is totally contradictory.

Very well, so let it be: but then we want to know who directs these forces; it is not we, for we do not know them. Hence it must be some being who knows them, whose knowledge, therefore, must be higher than ours. But this being is invisible; hence neither man nor woman; who then can it be?

Nature? The atheist's nature, nature without God, nature manipulating and managing herself in her own person? What! would nature contradict and violate herself? And why? Just because someone has prayed to *somebody else* than herself?

For in any other case she does not run counter to herself, but follows her regular course. Hence, if she is to stultify herself, we must invoke God or the Virgin—otherwise nothing happens—and we may pray to her as we pray to Our Lady of Lourdes, and she will remain as inert and insensible as ever. You can easily try, if you will. Venerate her as dithyrambically as you please, invoke her in any way you can think of, and see whether the cancer which is gnawing you will disappear!

Thus these arguments cannot stand, and we are driven to fall back upon some commanding power which she obeys—that is to say, upon God and the Virgin.

But how are we to get the sure existence of such divine dynamics admitted by those who—it is only right to confess it—have every possible motive for denying it?

These Apparitions of the Virgin, attested as they are by such unheard-of acts, are indeed very disquieting for many people, if you come to think of it.

Take, for instance, the case of a man, not a rascal with a corrupted conscience, but an honest fellow who has not the faith or has lost it, just as many others have done, on leaving college, when the increasing power of the senses is making itself felt. If he remembers the teaching of the catechism, he regards it as childish, and is almost astounded that he could ever have been naïve enough to believe it. Moreover, he observes that the few practising Catholics of his acquaintance are more stupid than the rest—and, what is worse, that they are no better than himself—and then his position is settled: religion is all right for the weak-minded and for women and children; every man of education and sense must shake himself free of it; and his soul goes soundly to sleep and he enjoys himself without let or hindrance. He is incapable of doing any downright bad action; he may be, if you will, charitable, but has what we call his "weak point"; he is fond of a free life and of women.

And now it is roughly and bluntly brought home to him, and that by those upon whose good sense he can rely, that the Virgin is working miracles at Lourdes. Well then, She exists! And if She exists, Christ is God, and, as surely as thread follows needle, he has to acknowledge that the teaching of the catechism, which he thought so childish, is not so; then, the Church and all her dogmas are binding . . .

And here his trouble begins. If he hearkens to his conscience, he has to give up a host of pleasures in this world, turn his life upside down at the feet of a priest, and, if he is unmarried, live a life of chastity. If he does not do so, owing to human respect and cowardice, he is in a permanent state of simmering uneasiness and self-reproach.

The miraculous, in short, sounds the passing knell of earthly passion; one can see why people won't have it!

And so our honest fellow prefers to blindfold himself, and to hear and know nothing. How many of this type have I met! They had succeeded in concocting for themselves a certain sort of belief, resting chiefly upon negations and enabling them to live as they liked; and these folks did not even wish to be dislodged from it by Spiritualism, for they dreaded the reality of the supernatural of the *table d'hôte* or table-turning variety for fear of being driven to think of the other kind; they had settled down, quite placidly, in their lives—and, besides, what a business it all was! If they came to be convinced of the divinity of the Church, they would have to own that they had been mistaken and to become the laughing-stock of their friends!

Moreover, it matters little to sceptics of this stamp whether the arguments against Lourdes be sound or futile; they have not the least desire to go into them; they take refuge behind them as a wind-screen to shelter them from being bothered with further arguments.

This pusillanimity explains why Dr. Boissarie's clinic, though thrown so widely open to everyone, is so little frequented by unbelievers. It has against it what may be called the hatred of fear, of the fear of the Faith.

To come back to Lourdes itself: it is, I repeat, a place both repulsive and divine, but it is only right to make trial of it by personal experience.

As for the sick, as soon as science declares that it can do no more for their relief, they do well to go there; for if the Virgin does not hearken to their prayers, She will repay them for the toil and the fatigue of the journey by bestowing upon them the blessings of resignation and comfort; and is not that a great deal? As for pilgrims in good health, if they are lovers of the intimate and the artistic, they must be prepared to suffer, for they cannot help being stirred to holy wrath when they see the diabolical horrors of ugliness that are being inflicted upon us by the degeneracy of churchmen; but the Madonna will give them in exchange a wonderful vision of moral Beauty, and of spiritual Beauty illumined by the raptures of Faith and Charity.

And after all, who knows what She keeps in store for her visitors?

✳

And now, on the point of taking leave of her, looking at the portrait, hitherto unknown, but which, since Bernadette's revelations, stands for her likeness, I say to myself:

"After all, dear Mother, how strange you appear! Here, to begin with, I cannot recognise you in the form of a little girl before the time of Bethlehem and Golgotha; you are so different from the images of Our Lady of the Middle Ages and even from those set before us by the centuries that followed!

"But when I reflect thereon, I understand this avatar of your effigy, the freshness of its pose, the renewal of its features.

"The liturgy of the feast of the Immaculate Conception constantly speaks of Eve; it sets one of you against the other and mingles your names together: its office of Matins appears to be the unfolding of the *Mutans Evae nomen* of your Vesper Hymn.

"You are plainly She who moved under various names and figures through the pages of the Old Testament. You are—without Crib and without Cross—the Virgin who is older than the Gospels.

"You are the daughter of the imperishable Plan, the Wisdom born before all the ages.

"You yourself have declared in the Epistle of your Mass: 'The Lord possessed me in the beginning of his ways, before he made anything, from the beginning. I was set up from eternity, and of old, before the earth was made. The depths were not as yet, and I was already conceived.'

"Thus, from a newer point of view, you are the oldest Virgin of all. You are, in any case, the Wise Virgin who discloses herself at Lourdes, more than anywhere else, as the substitute for the foolish virgin, for poor Eve.

"Just as she was framed of a body taken from a lump of earth, alive and yet untainted, You, too, were reformed of flesh unspotted by original sin.

"The Immaculate Conception brings us back through the Bible, to the age of Chaos in Genesis, and thence as we retrace our steps to Eden, I cannot help my thoughts turning to Eve, now among the saints, and disconsolate with the sorrows of her descendants and with the frightful diseases that they never would have known but for her sin, as she stands there close to You, and begs you to repay the debts she owes to these, her poor unhappy children, and to heal them. . . .

"And you, though you wrought no miracles while living here on earth, You work them now both for her and for yourself, O Light of goodness that knows no setting, O Haven of the miserable and weeping, Mary most compassionate, Mother of pity!"

A PARTIAL LIST OF SNUGGLY BOOKS

JASON ROLFE *An Archive of Human Nonsense*
BRIAN STABLEFORD (editor)
Decadence and Symbolism: A Showcase Anthology
BRIAN STABLEFORD (editor) *The Snuggly Satyricon*
BRIAN STABLEFORD *The Insubstantial Pageant*
BRIAN STABLEFORD *Spirits of the Vasty Deep*
BRIAN STABLEFORD *The Truths of Darkness*
COUNT ERIC STENBOCK *Love, Sleep & Dreams*
COUNT ERIC STENBOCK *Myrtle, Rue & Cypress*
COUNT ERIC STENBOCK *The Shadow of Death*
COUNT ERIC STENBOCK *Studies of Death*
MONTAGUE SUMMERS *The Bride of Christ and Other Fictions*
MONTAGUE SUMMERS *Six Ghost Stories*
GILBERT-AUGUSTIN THIERRY *The Blonde Tress and The Mask*
GILBERT-AUGUSTIN THIERRY *Reincarnation and Redemption*
DOUGLAS THOMPSON *The Fallen West*
TOADHOUSE *Gone Fishing with Samy Rosenstock*
TOADHOUSE *Living and Dying in a Mind Field*
RUGGERO VASARI *Raun*
JANE DE LA VAUDÈRE *The Demi-Sexes and The Androgynes*
JANE DE LA VAUDÈRE *The Double Star and Other Occult Fantasies*
JANE DE LA VAUDÈRE *The Mystery of Kama and Brahma's Courtesans*
JANE DE LA VAUDÈRE *The Priestesses of Mylitta*
JANE DE LA VAUDÈRE *Syta's Harem and Pharaoh's Lover*
JANE DE LA VAUDÈRE *Three Flowers and The King of Siam's Amazon*
JANE DE LA VAUDÈRE *The Witch of Ecbatana and The Virgin of Israel*
AUGUSTE VILLIERS DE L'ISLE-ADAM *Isis*
RENÉE VIVIEN AND HÉLÈNE DE ZUYLEN DE NYEVELT
Faustina and Other Stories
RENÉE VIVIEN *Lilith's Legacy*
RENÉE VIVIEN *A Woman Appeared to Me*
TERESA WILMS MONTT *In the Stillness of Marble*
TERESA WILMS MONTT *Sentimental Doubts*
KAREL VAN DE WOESTIJNE *The Dying Peasant*

CPSIA information can be obtained
at www.ICGtesting.com
Printed in the USA
BVHW042016120223
658283BV00010B/949